LEARNING UNDER STRESS:

children of single parents and the schools

by
Margaret Barnwell Hargreaves

Jo Sanders, Project Director

Women's Action Alliance
and
The Scarecrow Press, Inc.
Metuchen, N.J., & London
1991

This book is based on a research project supported by the John D. and Catherine T. MacArthur Foundation.

British Library Cataloguing-in-Publication data available

Library of Congress Cataloging-in-Publication Data

Hargreaves, Margaret Barnwell.
  Learning under stress : children of single parents and the schools / by Margaret Barnwell Hargreaves.
      p.   cm.
  Includes bibliographical references (p.   ) and index.
  ISBN 0-8108-2287-3
  1. Children of single parents—Education—United States. 2. Children of divorced parents—Education—United States.
  I. Women's Action Alliance. II. Title.
    LC5159.3.U6H37   1991
    370.19'34—dc 20   90-36579

CONTENTS

PREFACE

The origin of *Learning Under Stress* was an informal conversation among several staff members at Women's Action Alliance about our children and their schools. As we talked we began to realize that those of us who are single parents had problems dealing with schools that our coupled counterparts did not. One reported her daughter's sadness when the class made Father's Day cards. Another told us that her son's school problems, according to his teacher, had to be due to his "broken" family status. A third said that as an unmarried mother she felt looked down upon at school. We wondered about the effect of these difficulties on our children.

These incidents, small but emblematic, eventually precipitated broader discussions at Women's Action Alliance about what happens to single-parent children in schools. We knew it was an issue of special concern to women: most single parents *are* women. We had many questions. Is the academic performance of single-parent children different from that of coupled-parent children? What about their school behavior? Do single-parent children bring extra stresses from home into school? Do teachers help with these stresses or unknowingly add to them? Do curriculum materials show all kinds of families or just one? Are single parents involved in their children's education at the same rate that coupled parents are? In short, does it matter that some children come from single-parent homes? If so, how? And what can schools do about it?

These are some of the questions *Learning Under Stress* was written to answer. Women's Action Alliance is grateful to the John D. and Catherine T. MacArthur Foundation for its

support of the research project that led to the publication of
this book.

Jo Sanders, Project Director
Single Parents and the Schools Project
Women's Action Alliance
November 1989

Chapter One:

INTRODUCTION

In recent years the popular press has dramatized the lower academic achievement and higher drop-out rates of children from "broken homes" as compared with children from "intact families," using terms which imply that family circumstances are much at fault for dramatic educational differences between children from one-parent and two-parent homes. Millions of children, *over 50 percent of all children born since 1983, will spend some of their youth in a one-parent household.* Are these children at much higher risk for academic failure because they live with one parent instead of two? If an academic achievement gap exists between one-parent and two-parent children, the ramifications for educators are enormous.

The Children of Single Parents and the Schools Project has examined the existence and possible sources of single-parent children's academic troubles. The Project's research focused on two central questions: Is the one-parent family structure a broken, dysfunctional system which produces problem students? Do school practices discriminate against non-traditional families in ways that contribute to the educational differences between single-parent and two-parent students? These questions imply very different solutions to the academic problems of single-parent children.

This book reports the findings of the Children of Single Parents and the Schools Project, a four-month research study conducted by the Women's Action Alliance with the support of the John D. and Catherine T. MacArthur Foundation. The Project studied the school experiences of children from one-parent families in order to learn whether these children have problems that are different from the school problems of children from two-parent households. As we discovered, academic differences do exist. We then examined the potential causes of these problems, and the types of actions schools can take to help these children academically.

The Women's Action Alliance, a national organization which provides educational programs on a wide range of gender equity issues (including non-sexist classroom teaching techniques, computer equity in schools for girls, and training women for non-traditional occupations), initiated this Project when it became concerned over the well-publicized school problems of children from single-parent families, families most often headed by women. If children lose out academically because they come from new, non-traditional kinds of families, then schools must change their practices to accommodate and educate these children as well as children from more traditional two-parent homes.

The Problem

The educational problems of single-parent children are becoming a greater concern as more children grow up in one-parent households. Today one-fourth of all households are headed by one parent. The number of such families has doubled since 1970. It is estimated that half of all children born in the 1980's will spend some time in a one-parent family. The Alliance is concerned that children from non-traditional families not fall behind their two-parent classmates in school because their needs as single-parent children go unrecognized.

One of the most striking characteristics of single-parent families is the extreme diversity found in their backgrounds and circumstances. One-parent families come from affluent suburban communities where divorced, professional couples may share joint custody of their teen-age children, and they come from poor, inner-city neighborhoods where young, never-married women may raise their pre-school age children in extended-family households. This diversity of family types and community resources complicates any research about single-parent families and the schools.

Recognizing this diversity, the Project has focused on elementary school-age children from families headed by women—widows, divorced, separated, or never-married mothers. These young, mother-only children are an important group to study for several reasons. Mother-only children tend to have more academic problems than other single-parent children, in large part because they are the poorest group of single-parent children. Second, school interventions tend to have the most long-term impact when targeted at young children; early childhood programs can most help set children "on the right track" or can help them from "going down the wrong path." Finally, single mothers may need the most help from schools when their children are young and most dependent.

Methodology

The Project collected information on four broad topic areas from a variety of sources. We first collected census data, demographic research, and descriptive studies of one-parent families. The goal was to find out how many single-parent families exist, and what their lives tend to be like. The Project looked at the differences as well as the similarities among the various types of one-parent families to see whether these families fit one image, as commonly thought, or whether important differences exist between family types. This information is presented in the next chapter: Who Are America's One-Parent Families?

Next, we reviewed the research literature and interviewed education experts to learn about the school performance of single-parent children, as compared with two-parent children, and about the factors which affect the school experiences of one-parent children. Relevant literature reviewed included books, book chapters, journal articles, and newspaper and magazine articles. This information is presented in the third chapter: How Does Life At Home Affect School Performance?

In order to learn what schools are currently doing for

single-parent families the Project used three sources of information. In addition to reviewing the research findings of experts and interviewing educators and representatives from single-parent organizations, the Project collected first-hand information through focus group interviews. With the assistance of two researchers from Harvard's Graduate School of Education, Barbara Miller and Judith Dorney, we conducted focus group interviews with New York metropolitan area single mothers, single-parent children, and elementary school teachers.

Specifically, we conducted three group interviews of single mothers: one group consisted of divorced, separated, and widowed mothers from Manhattan, Staten Island, and the Bronx; the second group was made up of never-married mothers from the same boroughs; and the third was a mixed group of single mothers from Brooklyn and Queens. The composition of these single-parent groups was 50 percent black and Hispanic women and 50 percent white women; all were middle- or low-income, and most were employed full-time. We also conducted three focus groups with mixed groups of eight-, nine- and ten-year-old single-parent children at three YMCA day camps, one camp on Manhattan's lower east side, one at a midtown Manhattan branch, and one at a Flatbush neighborhood branch in Brooklyn. In addition we brought together a group of elementary school teachers from Manhattan, the Bronx, and urban New Jersey to get their perspective. The children's interviews lasted 45 minutes on average, and the adults' interviews took approximately two hours to complete. The information we obtained from all these sources is presented in chapters four and five of this report.

A summary with recommendations forms the final chapter of this report. This chapter attempts to go beyond the lists of recommended school practices that are already printed in school guides for educators. We have expanded the list and offer guidelines for integrating these recommendations into a comprehensive school program for single-parent children. Below is a brief summary of the Project's findings and recommendations.

Summary of Project Findings

The Project uncovered serious school problems among many single-parent children. Research has found that *single-parent children tend to have a greater risk for poor academic achievement than children from two-parent families.* Life in a one-parent family often seems to harm a child's academic performance in school, reflected in lower grades, and seems to lessen a child's total educational attainment, reflected in higher drop-out rates for single-parent children.

Popular wisdom often blames the academic problems these children have on their family situations, on the fact that they come from "broken homes" or that they have lost one parent. Such explanations assign all of the blame on the children's families and none on the school systems responsible for educating the children. The Project looked beyond the "broken family" stereotype into the realities of one-parent family life to learn what factors cause many of the children from these families to fall behind their classmates and eventually to drop out of school.

We found that both family conditions and school practices contribute to the problems that single-parent children have in school. Many school practices assume that students come from two-parent families, not recognizing that children from one-parent families often have emotional and economic problems not experienced by most two-parent children. In many schools these assumptions have created an environment in which single-parent children rarely receive the sensitivity and attention that they need in order to succeed. To date, few schools have modified their practices to accommodate one-parent children. School attitudes, parent/teacher conference schedules, curriculum materials, classroom discussions, and other student policies must be adjusted to meet the unique needs of one-parent families.

Few researchers have studied the reasons for the gap between single-parent student needs and school services. Excellent school guides offering suggestions on how schools can better serve single-parent children have been available since the early 1980's, but relatively few schools have taken the guides' recommendations to heart and changed their practices. This book suggests ways in which single parents and schools can work together to bridge this gap.

Recommendations

1. **Sensitivity Towards One-Parent Families:** Single-parent children and their parents require respect and sensitivity from school personnel regarding their family circumstances. We recommend training programs for teachers, counselors, and administrators that teach them about the one-parent families in their schools and help them to correct potential prejudices about these families.

2. **Early Warning System:** Many one-parent families experience crises, such as death or divorce, during which the children involved tend to suffer academically and can lose ground in the long run if their problems are nòt spotted and addressed promptly. We recommend that schools develop information systems to detect and correct academic problems as early as possible.

3. **Family Support:** Some effective school-based single-parent family support group programs have been developed for families that are going through a divorce. These programs help children cope with their family problems and reduce their divorce-related problems in school, and teach single parents how to cope effectively with their new family situation. We recommend these school-based support groups for one-parent families that need this extra support and assistance.

4. **Child Care:** Many single parents have the double burden of being the sole breadwinner as well as the sole caretaker for their families, and lack the resources to find or afford child care for their children outside of school. American teachers consider the lack of child care for school-age children to be a prime source of school problems. We recommend that, in addition to offering child care for all school events, schools and communities should work together to provide affordable child-care programs before school, after school, and during school vacations.

5. **Classroom Practices:** Finally, one-parent children often feel "different" and unwelcome at school, emotions that are reinforced by the under-representation of one-parent families in school curricula and activities. We recommend that schools develop classroom materials which accurately reflect the family backgrounds of the children enrolled. We also recommend that teachers help single parents become more involved in their children's education by offering parent involvement activities specifically geared for single-parent families.

Chapter Two:

WHO ARE AMERICA'S ONE-PARENT FAMILIES?

The characteristics of the nation's elementary and secondary school student population are undergoing considerable change. *Today's students are more likely than ever before to come from minority groups, from poor families, and from one-parent families* (Stedman, 1987). Among the most dramatic and far-reaching demographic changes in the last two decades has been the rapid increase in the number of single-parent families: families comprised of one parent with one or more children under the age of eighteen. This chapter will describe the one-quarter of American families which are headed by one parent, their rapid rise, and their family characteristics.

Growth of One-Parent Families

Rapid Increase. *Over the last two decades the number of one-parent families with children under 18 has more than doubled,* increasing from 3.8 million families in 1970 to 9.2 million families in 1987. Fifteen million children live in these single-parent families, almost one-fourth (24.6 percent) of the 61.1 million children under the age of 18 in the United States living with one or both parents. These single-parent children also constitute one-fourth (24.3 percent) of all American elementary and middle school students, children aged 6 through 14 (Norton & Glick, 1986).

In contrast, as Table 1 indicates, the number of two-parent families with children under the age of eighteen has declined by 2.7 percent since 1970 (U.S. Department of

TABLE 1
Growth of Families and Subfamilies with Children Under 18 from 1970 to 1987

(numbers in thousands)	1970				1987				Amount Change	Percent Change
	All	White	Black	Hispanic	All	White	Black	Hispanic		
All Families & Subfamilies with Children under 18	29,483	26,264	2,931	NA	34,232	28,180	4,963	3,165	+4,759	16
Total Two-Parent Families	25,687	23,674	1,965	NA	25,006	22,075	2,059	2,115	−681	−3
Total Father-Only Families	383	299	82	NA	1,107	914	157	123	+724	189
Total Mother-Only Families	3,413	2,344	1,046	NA	8,119	5,184	2,747	927	+4,706	138
Separated Mother Families	1,377	806	559	NA	1,725	1,109	562	288	+348	25
Divorced Mother Families	1,104	929	168	NA	3,308	2,708	534	275	+2,204	199
Widowed Mother Families	685	534	147	NA	511	352	139	55	−174	−25
Never-Married Mother Families	247	74	171	NA	2,575	1,015	1,512	310	+2,328	942

"Families" refers to two or more related individuals, one of whom is the householder, all residing together. "Sub-families" refers to two or more related individuals living in the household of relatives or other non-related individuals. All statistics are from the Bureau of the Census, Household and Family Characteristics: March 1970, and 1987. Numbers are not available for the Hispanic population for 1970.

Commerce, 1987 & 1970). Thus, the overall proportion of one-parent families in the United States has risen dramatically, from one out of every eight families in 1970 to over one in four families today. This change in the proportion of one-parent families can be seen in Graph 1 (U.S. Department of Commerce, various years). The rate of increase of one-parent families has begun to slow recently, possibly because as the baby boom generation ages fewer women are entering their child bearing years. In the future, the total number of one-parent families will continue to grow, although at a slower pace (*Single Parents . . . ,* 1983).

Mother-Headed Families. As Table 2 indicates, women head 8.1 million of the 9.2 million one-parent families, a substantial majority (88 percent) (U.S. Department of Commerce, 1987). Single fathers headed 1.1 million families as of 1987, almost triple the number of father-only families recorded in 1970. As more divorced men gain custody of their children, father-only families have been growing at a slightly faster rate than mother-only families. However, the total number of father-only families has not increased fast enough to appreciably alter the overall proportion of families maintained by men (Norton & Glick, 1986). Consequently, the proportion of mother-only families among all single-parent families has not significantly changed over the last 20 years.

A substantial minority of single parents and their children (21 percent in 1987) do not maintain their own households but live in the households of relatives or non-related individuals (Norton & Glick, 1986). Studies which discuss single-parent households usually fail to include the 2 million single parents and their children who share living quarters with others. Over 90 percent of these 2 million "subfamilies" are headed by women. Most often they are young, black, unmarried mothers who live with their children in a larger family grouping. Not counting these "subfamilies," one-parent households with children under the age of eighteen totaled approximately 7.9 million in 1987.

Reasons for the Increase. High rates of separation and divorce, and a higher proportion of births by unmarried women, account for the substantial growth of single-parent families. This section will outline the trends in these marriage

Graph 1: Families with Children

Percent of families with own children under 18, by type of family: 1950 to 1985

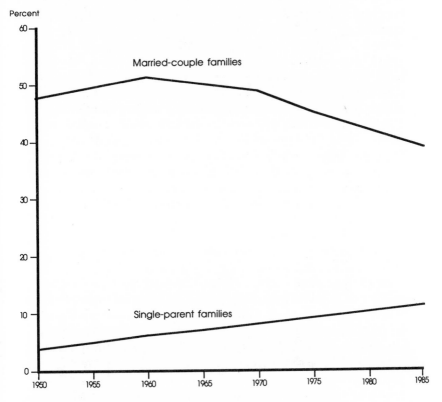

SOURCE: U.S. Department of Commerce, Bureau of the Census, Current Population Reports, Series P-20, Household and Family Characteristics, various years.

While the proportion of married-couple families with their own children under 18 declined between 1970 and 1985, the proportion of single-parent families has grown.

TABLE 2
Families and Sub-families[a] with Children Under 18, 1987

(numbers in thousands)	Two-Parent Families	Single Fathers	Single Mothers[b]	Separated	Divorced	Widowed	Never-Married
Total							
Families = 34,242	25,006	1,107	8,119	1,725	3,308	511	2,575
= 100%	73.0%	3.2%	23.7%	5.0%	9.7%	1.5%	7.5%
White							
Families = 28,180	22,075	914	5,184	1,109	2,708	352	1,015
= 100%	78.3%	3.2%	18.4%	3.9%	9.6%	1.2%	3.6%
Black							
Families = 4,964	2,059	157	2,747	562	534	139	1,512
= 100%	41.5%	3.2%	55.3%	11.3%	10.8%	2.8%	30.5%
Hispanic							
Families = 3,165	2,115	123	927	288	275	55	310
(any race) = 100%	66.8%	3.9%	29.3%	9.1%	8.7%	1.7%	9.8%

[a] According to the U.S. Census, a sub-family refers to two or more related individuals residing in the home of another related or non-related family.
[b] The Census Bureau does not collect information on custody of children. For this reason, we are unable to report on custody of two separated parents. U.S. Department of Commerce, Bureau of the Census. "Marital Status and Living Arrangements: March 1987," Current Population Reports, Series P-20, No. 423.

and family formation patterns and their impact on single-parent family statistics (Zill & Rogers, 1988).

Although the divorce rate has been rising since the middle of the nineteenth century, there was a steep increase in the frequency of divorce during the 1960's and 1970's. As the divorce rate rose, so did the number of children affected. The number of children whose parents became legally divorced has climbed from less than 500,000 children per year in 1960 to more than a million children per year by 1975 (Zill & Rogers, 1988).

Although the divorce rate began to fall slightly in 1979, dropping 6 percent between 1979 and 1984, by 1984 there were still more than one million children whose parents became divorced in a given year (Hetherington, Hagan & Anderson, in press). The divorce rate stabilized through 1985 and then dropped again between 1985 and 1986. Even if the rate continues to decline, it still remains at a very high level. *As of March 1987 almost two-thirds (64 percent) of all single-parent families were the result of separation or divorce.*

The fastest growing group of single parents is never-married mothers, a group which has increased over tenfold since 1970—from 247,000 families to 2.6 million families in 1987. This increase is caused, in part, by a greater proportion of women bearing children outside of marriage. While births to all women have declined, births to unmarried women have remained constant; the result has been a proportional rise in the number of children born out of wedlock. In 1950 only 4 percent of all births were to unmarried mothers. By 1985 births to unmarried mothers accounted for an estimated 22 percent of all babies born in the United States (Zill & Rogers, 1988).

More children are also being raised by never-married mothers. As of 1987, 7.5 percent of all families were led by never-married mothers, almost one-third (28 percent) of all single-parent families. The number of never-married families has continued to grow in the 1980's, but there are indications that the rate of growth of these families has started to decline.

For much of history large numbers of children experienced the loss of one or both parents, usually through the death of a parent. But widowhood has gradually given way to divorce as the major cause of single-parent families (Norton & Glick, 1986). Presently in the United States, widow-headed families constitute by far the smallest group (5.5 percent) of single-parent families, and only 1.5 percent of all families with children under eighteen. The proportion of widow-led families to all families is expected to remain constant; it would change only if there were a disproportionate change in men's and women's life expectancies or if an event such as war caused many fathers of young children to die prematurely.

Lifetime Prevalence of One-Parent Families. The numbers presented in the preceding sections reflect the number of one-parent families at a specific point in 1987. These 1987 numbers are snapshots of a given time which do not fully reveal the number of parents and children who ever spend time in a one-parent family. In the United States marriage is a fairly impermanent state through which many families pass. Eighty-five percent of unmarried mothers eventually marry, the vast majority (90 percent in the 1970's) of divorced custodial parents remarry, and family units break up as children grow up and leave home (Weitzman, 1985).

As a result, many more children live with one parent at some point than are captured by the census data in a given year, and the one-parent families counted by the Census Bureau one year may not be the same one-parent families counted by the Census Bureau a year later. As a result, these "point in time" statistics grossly underestimate the actual number of children who spend some time in a one-parent family. According to U.S. Census Bureau estimates, close to 60 percent of the children born in 1983 will not spend their entire childhood living with both natural parents (U.S. Department of Commerce, 1983).

For most parents and children, divorce is only one in a series of family transitions that follow marital separation (Hetherington, 1987). After divorce, a child might remain in the family home with one parent, then move to a new home if custody is granted to the other parent, and eventually become part of a larger step-family if the custodial parent remarries. *Divorce involving children is most likely to occur when the children are between the ages of five and twelve* (Stedman, 1987). Since divorce is frequently followed by remarriage, and more than half of all remarriages end in divorce, many children are exposed to a succession of family types by the time they are eighteen. Overall, it is estimated that one in ten children will face divorce, remarriage of the custodial parent, and then a second divorce from the step-parent (Pedro-Carroll, 1986).

A decade ago, researchers argued that it might be more appropriate to think of the time, four years on average, that a child spent in a single-parent household as a transitory period between life in a non-divorced family and life in a step-family. More recently researchers have estimated that the length of this transition period has become considerably longer, averaging five years for whites and seven years for blacks in 1984 (Garfinkel & McLanahan, 1986). The rate of remarriage has also begun to decrease in the 1970's. Based on 1985 patterns, only 70 percent of currently divorced men and women will eventually remarry (Chase-Lansdale & Hetherington, in press). From the child's perspective, these transition years represent a long period of time, and a significant portion of their childhood.

Racial and Ethnic Characteristics

Some groups of children are much more likely than others to live in a single-parent family, as is shown in Graph 2. Although two-thirds of all one-parent families are white, blacks are greatly overrepresented among one-parent families. Although 27 percent of all families are led by one parent, Census Bureau figures show that 58.5 percent of all black families are headed by one parent (see Table 2). Hispanic families are also overrepresented; single parents head 33.2 percent of all Hispanic families. Conversely, whites account for a disproportionately small share of single parents; only 21.6 percent of white families are one-parent families. This information indicates that *black families are nearly three times more likely than white families to be headed by one parent.*

These census figures should be viewed with some caution, however. Some small research studies which recounted the population of certain urban neighborhoods found that

Graph 2: Children of Single Parents

Percent of own children living in single-parent families, by race of family head: 1965 to 1985

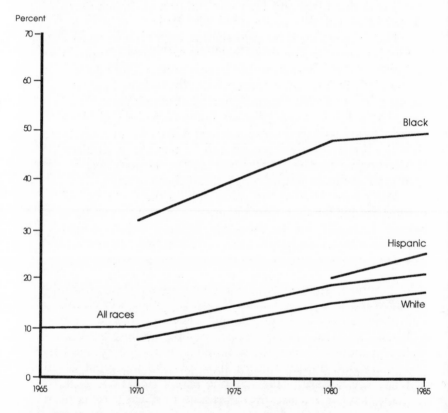

Percent

SOURCE: U.S. Department of Commerce, Bureau of the Census, Current Population Reports, Series P-20, Household and Family Characteristics, various years.

The percentage of children living in single-parent families is increasing. In 1985, 21 percent of all children lived in single-parent families compared to 10 percent in 1965. More than one-half of black children lived in single-parent homes in 1985.

census takers undercounted black male heads of households by an astounding 20 to 34 percent. It is not known how inaccurate the overall census figures are, but some undercount of young black men is certain. Some researchers speculate that residents' fear of detection by welfare eligibility workers may partly cause these undercounts. Despite this, it is still true that black and Hispanic children are much more likely to live with one parent than with both.

The proportion of families sharing each type of marital status also varies among these three ethnic groups. Divorced and separated mothers form the largest portion of white single-parent families, while never-married mothers head the largest portion of both Hispanic and black single-parent families. The greatest disparity exists between white and black never-married mothers; these mothers head 19.6 percent of all white female-headed families and 55 percent of all black female-headed families. As we will see in the next section, each kind of family has its own unique characteristics.

Many have debated the cause behind the rapid rise of mother-headed families. Some blame the increase on welfare benefit increases for mother-only families, while others blame the rise on the break-down of "traditional" family values. Recent research has found that increases in welfare benefits are not the major cause in the growth of mother-only families (Garfinkel & McLanahan, 1986). For middle-income (usually white) groups, increases in employment opportunities and greater economic independence for women have been the most important causes. For low-income (mostly black) groups, increases in poverty and declines in employment opportunities for unskilled men, which make these men less eligible marriage partners, seem to be the main factors behind the increase in mother-only families.

Types of One-Parent Families

Like two-parent families, each one-parent family is unique and has its own strengths and weaknesses. These families live everywhere: in large cities, in suburbs, in small towns, and in rural areas. They are also found among all ethnic groups, religions, backgrounds, and income levels. These families share many emotional, social, financial, and practical challenges as one parent takes over both roles as provider and nurturer—duties traditionally shared by two parents. Yet there are some important distinctions among various types of single-parent families: families led by never-married mothers, separated mothers, divorced mothers, widowed mothers, and single fathers.

Never-married Mothers. Never-married mothers, now 28 percent of all single parents, include women who adopt, give birth to, or have as a ward, one or more children. They span the social spectrum from young teen-age mothers to older professional women who choose to start families on their own. Researcher Judith Worell argues that age is an important determinant of the social stigma these women face, with adolescents receiving the largest share of social isolation and community punishment for rearing children outside of marriage (Worell, 1986).

Never-married mothers are by far the poorest group of single parents; they have an average annual income of $6,676 in 1987—one-sixth the $37,864 average income of two-parent households. As Table 3 indicates, these mothers, the youngest single-parent group, have completed the least education, are least likely to be in the labor force, and are most likely to be dependent on government assistance (Zill & Rogers, 1988). Fewer than half of these unmarried mothers have finished high school (though some of them may still be in high school or are of high-school age). Those never-married mothers in the labor force also suffer the highest unemployment rate of all single mothers. These mothers tend to spend more time at home with their children than other single parents, though this may have more to do with their personal backgrounds, present joblessness, and lack of social and career opportunities than with their never-married status.

Separated Mothers. For parents and children, marital separation marks the beginning of the divorce process, a sequence of changes in life circumstances that can extend over a period of many years. For most families, divorce means that the father sets up a separate residence and the mother becomes head of the household. At the start of these unfamiliar

Table 3: Education and Employment Status of Families with Children Under 18 Years, 1987

	2 - Parent Families	Single Fathers	Single Mothers				
			Separated	Divorced	Widowed	Never Married	All Single Mothers
Number of families	25,006,000	1,107,000	1,725,000	3,308,000	511,000	2,575,000	8,119,000
Percent	73 %	3.2 %	5.0 %	9.7 %	1.5 %	7.5 %	23.7 %
Mean number of children	1.84	1.45	1.87	1.61	1.61	1.74	1.74
Percent of 6 - 14 year olds	73 %	2.7 %	5.4 %	9.8 %	1.5 %	5.0 %	24.3 %
Education							
Percent of parents who are high school graduates	82.7 %	75.5 %	62.3 %	79.2 %	58.5 %	56.6 %	67.1 %
Percent of parents who are college graduates	13.1 %	7.6 %	4.7 %	6.3 %	6.2 %	1.6 %	4.5 %
Employment							
Percent of parents who are employed full time	82.7 % one 52.1 % both	72.8 %	35.7 %	57 %	30.9 %	24.6 %	40.5 %
Percent of parents who are employed part-time	4.8 %	8.4 %	13.4 %	13.3 %	16.3 %	9.1 %	12.3 %
Percent of parents who are unemployed	4.6 %	9.8 %	10.3 %	6.8 %	5.7 %	14.4 %	9.9 %
Percent of parents in labor force	92.1 %	90.9 %	59.5 %	77.1 %	52.9 %	48.1 %	62.7 %
Age of largest percentage of parents	35 - 44	35 - 44	35 - 44	35 - 44	55 - 64	25 - 29	35 - 44

SOURCE: U.S. Department of Commerce, Bureau of the Census, 1987

roles, separated parents often feel a mixture of relief, hurt, resentment, and also a sense of loss over absent family routines. Most separated parents take over a year to resolve their emotional storms and over two years to adjust fully to their new situation (Knight, 1980).

The period of separation includes many changes for mothers, especially for those women who had stayed at home during the marriage to take care of their children. At separation these mothers often go back to school, enter the work force, change jobs, or increase their working hours in order to take on the responsibility of financially providing for their children. Economically, this can be an especially stressful time for mothers who must maintain their households and support their children before the divorce courts award them any child support or alimony payments.

For many women and children the consequences of marital separation mean swift downward mobility, both economically and socially. *In the first year of divorce, women and their children experience a 73 percent decline in their standard of living,* while men experience an average 42 percent rise (Weitzman, 1985). Such downward mobility is associated with poorer quality housing, less safe neighborhoods, changes in employment, enrollment in welfare, and a loss of social networks and support (Hetherington, 1987). Separation entails a series of stresses which are difficult to handle in the short run and can also be harmful to families in the long run.

These social, emotional, and financial upheavals distinguish separated mothers from other single parents. After never-married mothers, separated mothers have the lowest annual income ($10,419), the highest unemployment rate (10.3 percent), and are least likely to have finished college. Separated mothers make up 18.7 percent of all single parents.

Divorced Mothers. Divorced mothers form the largest group of single parents, totaling over one-third (35.9 percent) of all single parents. As a group, divorced mothers share somewhat better circumstances than separated mothers. This happens because many of these women have successfully passed through the initial crisis stages of marital dissolution or because women of low socioeconomic status do not obtain formal divorces as often as others. Within two years of the divorce many women have made significant adjustments by reorganizing their lives, accepting the divorce, and re-orienting their identities as single parents. More divorced mothers are in the labor force, have finished college and work full-time than any other single parent group except for single fathers. Still, in one study 70 percent of the divorced women reported being perpetually worried "about making ends meet." Accordingly, divorced women report more stress and less satisfaction with their lives than any other group of Americans (Weitzman, 1985).

Most divorced women have to face a situation familiar to many separated mothers: the other parent is a physical and emotional reality in their lives and the lives of their children. Although joint custody arrangements have become common in some states, most divorced women still have sole custody of their children. In families where sole custody is granted, unfortunately the children usually have little contact with their non-custodial parent, and the parents rarely communicate about the raising of their children (Zill & Rogers, 1988).

In some states such as California, and among some groups, especially middle- and upper-income groups, more families are choosing to share custody of their children. As one teacher explained in a focus group interview, these joint-custody situations can seem more like "double parent" families. Both parents may want individual parent/teacher conferences, for example. The Census Bureau does not track joint-custody families, as children are assigned to only one legal residence. In reality the living arrangements are often more creative. Children may divide their time between two homes, or sometimes parents can take turns in a common home where the children live permanently.

Widowed Mothers. Experts agree that the loss of one's spouse through death or divorce is probably one of life's most stressful events and requires the greatest readjustment. Although death and divorce are often considered comparable crises involving the loss of an important family member, an important distinction remains. In the case of a parent's death, the departure of the parent is final. In the situation of divorce, the absent parent still lives and plays some role in the family.

A widow must come to terms with the death of her husband, while adapting to life as a single parent. Depression is a normal response to a spouse's death. Her grief and guilt may or may not be mixed with feelings of relief, resentment, anger, and separation anxiety that are common to other single parents. A woman with young children may also feel shameful about her widowhood at the "wrong" age. Although after divorce many women experience euphoria, greater independence, self-esteem, and some disappointment over a "failed" marriage, widows generally experience an unwanted, irreparable, and uncontrollable feeling of loss (Amato, 1987).

Contrary to popular belief, the sympathy and support that widows receive is often short-lived, after which widowed mothers share many of the same challenges faced by other single parents (Amato, 1987). But these women are often less financially disadvantaged than divorced mothers for several reasons: they do not have to split the marital assets, many are entitled to life insurance payments and survivors' Social Security benefits, and many retain their family homes. The 1987 Census Bureau figures show that widowed mothers have an average annual income of $16,897, a much higher income than any other group of single mothers. Possibly because these women form the oldest group of single mothers, they have the smallest number of young children, only 1.5 percent of all children aged 6 through 14 (Moore, 1987).

Single Fathers. Single fathers head over one million single-parent families, a number which has been growing in recent years as more fathers find it acceptable and even desirable to care for their children on their own. More men are now willing to accept custody or to fight for it. Fathers with custody face pressures similar to all single parents: maintaining a household, caring for children, and holding a job. However, single fathers get more assistance from friends, neighbors, their children, and paid housekeepers, and are more accustomed than custodial mothers to outside employment (Hetherington, Camara, & Featherman, 1983; Weiss, 1987). Single mothers have reported observing single fathers receiving the kinds of support and help they themselves wish they had (Arendell, 1984). In the Project's focus group interviews, for example, several mothers mentioned situations in which school personnel were more hesitant to call single fathers at work to take their children out of school than to call working single mothers for the same reason. Fathers who really want and gain custody also seem better able to combine responsibilities than fathers who do not want custody.

Children who live with fathers after divorce seldom encounter the stresses associated with limited finances that children experience in mother-only families. Single-father families have an average annual income of $24,000, more than twice the average family income ($11,450) of single mothers. Single fathers tend to be more secure economically than single mothers, in part because the fathers tend to have had more education and are more likely to be in the labor force (Norton & Glick, 1986). Yet children living with single fathers are still relatively disadvantaged compared to children of two-parent families, in that single fathers tend to have less education and lower incomes than married fathers. The children in father-only families also tend to be male, older, and less likely to be black or Hispanic than children in mother-only families (Zill & Rogers, 1988).

Poverty in Mother-Only Families

The most striking difference between mother-only and father-only families is the difference in the economic resources of the two family types. *Fully 60 percent of the children living with their mothers are in poverty,* compared to 26 percent of those living with their fathers. In 1985, 66 percent of black children, over 70 percent of Hispanic children, and nearly half of all white children living in female-headed households lived in poverty. Single women and their dependent children are the poorest of all major demographic groups in the United States, regardless of how poverty is measured, and they are also the major welfare recipient group (Garfinkel & McLanahan, 1986).

The poverty rate for mother-headed families has always been high, not changing dramatically over the last fifteen years, as is shown in Graph 3. But relative to other groups

Graph 3: Children in Poverty

Percent of children under 18 living in poverty, by family status: 1960 to 1985

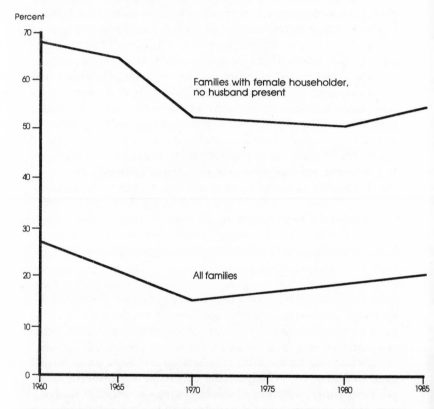

Percent

Families with female householder,
no husband present

All families

SOURCE: U.S. Department of Commerce, Bureau of the Census, Current Population Reports, Series P-20,"Characteristics of the Populations Below the Poverty Level", various years; and "Money Income and Poverty Status of Families and Persons in the United States", various years.

The proportion of children living in poverty declined significantly during the 1960's, but has risen since 1970. In 1985, about 20 percent of all children and 54 percent of children in female-headed families with no husband present lived in poverty.

such as the elderly and the disabled, the economic situation of mother-only families has actually worsened over the last two decades. The gap between mother-only families and other groups has widened in part because the living standards of other groups have improved.

Poverty also lasts longer among mother-only families and is more severe than for other families. In the 1970's the average time spent in poverty for children in mother-headed families was 7 years, compared to 4.6 years for children in two-parent families (Garfinkel & McLanahan, 1986). What causes such poverty among mother-only families? Researchers agree that a combination of societal factors tends to trap single mothers and their children in poverty and dependence (Garfinkel & McLanahan, 1986; Ellwood, 1988). These factors are:

- Inadequate child support from non-custodial fathers.
- Labor market difficulties of single mothers.
- Meager benefits from public assistance programs.

Lack of Child Support. In most mother-headed families the absent father contributes little or nothing to the family income. Only 40 percent of all white fathers and 19 percent of all black fathers pay child support. In the past, divorce courts tended to set minimal child support award levels, averaging per year $3,129 for white mothers and $1,698 for black mothers. Although the average annual court-ordered child support in 1982 was $2,460, the average annual amount actually received was $1,000 (Hetherington, 1987). This award, even when the father pays it, often leaves the wife and children in poverty. The women least likely to receive child support are those who need it most: women of color, women with little education, and never-married and separated women (Zill & Rogers, 1988).

Labor Market Difficulties. The major source of income for both two-parent and mother-only families is the earnings of the primary breadwinner. Because of differences in labor market participation and wages, women heading single-parent families earn only 35 percent as much as fathers in two-parent families. Single mothers tend to complete less formal education and enter the labor market later than married fathers because they have invested a considerable amount of time and energy caring for their children. As a result, these women are more likely to lack the work experience and job seniority to help them in time of layoffs or to qualify them for unemployment compensation (Garfinkel & McLanahan, 1986; Ellwood, 1988).

Sex discrimination in employment is a major labor market problem for single mothers that is not shared by men. Many women are questioned about their children on job interviews, an illegal practice which is still quite common. In addition, women continue to suffer substantial wage discrimination. Less than half of the male/female wage gap is due to differences in worker productivity (i.e., education, work experience, and skill level). Even when the occupations are comparable, women's salaries are 64 percent of men's salaries (Hetherington, 1987). It is argued that the rest of the wage gap between men and women is due to wage discrimination.

Full-time work or marriage are the only routes out of poverty and welfare for single parents, but even these are not always enough. According to poverty researcher David Ellwood, single mothers who work full-time are usually able to avoid poverty (Ellwood, 1988). However divorce expert Lenore Weitzman argues that one-third of the single mothers employed full-time cannot earn enough to enable them and their children to live above the poverty level (Weitzman, 1985).

Full-time work for a single mother seems worthwhile only if, being relatively well-educated and with few child care responsibilities, she can command a reasonably high salary and has modest child care costs. Accordingly, single mothers with young children are less likely to be in the labor force than married mothers, but single mothers are more likely to be in the labor force when their children are older. Despite these work obstacles, almost 41 percent of all single mothers work full-time year round, compared to 27 percent of all married mothers (Ellwood, 1988).

Inadequate Welfare Benefits. The single mothers who do not work full-time have few financial resources other than welfare. About 12 percent of single mothers work part-time while on welfare, though the added income usually means a cut in their welfare benefits (Ellwood, 1988). The rest of the non-working single mothers who do not depend on relatives for support rely on cash assistance through the federal/state program Aid to Families with Dependent Children (AFDC) and in-kind assistance programs such as Food Stamps. *In 1986, women family heads and their dependent children made up 80 percent of all AFDC recipients,* over half of all households receiving Food Stamps, almost all of the recipients of free or reduced school meals, and well over half of the non-elderly residents of public housing (Rodgers, 1986).

Even with assistance from more than one welfare program, the vast majority of AFDC families remain far below the poverty level. As a consequence, a substantial minority of female-headed families remain poor and dependent for long periods of time (Garfinkel & McLanahan, 1986). At least one-fourth of all single mothers will collect AFDC benefits for over ten years, even though they feel isolated and distrusted by welfare workers and are seen as abusers of government generosity despite their extreme poverty (Ellwood, 1988). Most women are still poor when they leave the welfare rolls.

Single-Parent Family Stresses. Economic problems may pose the greatest challenges for women who are single parents. *But all single mothers and fathers, regardless of income level, share several kinds of stresses,* including significant economic changes, the practical responsibilities of single parenting, and social isolation and loneliness. All single parents, except for never-married mothers, also share a difficult emotional adjustment period after the traumas of death, divorce, or separation (Schorr & Schorr, 1988). Without adequate backup support and resources, some custodial parents become physically and emotionally depleted. As Lisbeth Schorr says:

> All families rearing children need support, be it from friends, relatives, neighbors, or more organized sources. The job is simply too hard to handle alone. But for parents who are isolated, and beset by a multitude of other stresses, the stakes are higher and support can

prevent severe damage. . . A parent, especially a very
young one, who is raising a child alone, is in a particularly vulnerable position.

When faced with new or excessive demands and limited
resources, single parents often feel overwhelmed. Many divorced women report that they do not have the time or energy to deal competently with all the routine financial tasks,
household maintenance, child care, and occupational or social demands. These burdens can be mammoth, especially in
families of more than one child. What impacts do the special
circumstances of single-parent families have on children and
on their academic development? The next chapter will review
what researchers have found out about this question.

Chapter Three:

HOW DOES LIFE AT HOME AFFECT SCHOOL PERFORMANCE?

Chapter Two discussed the various types of one-parent families, and some of their common characteristics. In all these families, one parent typically takes on the entire daily responsibility of raising the children and preparing them for adulthood. In this chapter we will examine the impact that living in a one-parent family has on children. How well do the children in these families develop socially and intellectually? Do these children face any special psychological and intellectual risks because of their family status? These are important questions for teachers, school administrators, and education policy makers. If one-parent children have special needs, then schools must know what they are and meet those that are crucial to the children's academic and future occupational success.

Research Limitations

Early research focused on the absence of one parent (usually the father) as the critical difference between one-parent and two-parent families. The researchers paid little attention to the great diversity found among one-parent families, to their variations in life experiences, socioeconomic backgrounds, and the quality of parent/child relationships. For example, previous research on the impact of divorce assumed that divorce was a single, uniform event in which the father left the household, and that this event was inevitably harmful to children. More recent research has found the effects of divorce to be more moderate and more complex than previously assumed (Peterson, 1986). The impact of living in a one-parent family on children depends not only on the absence of the second parent, but hinges on many additional factors including (Hetherington, Camara, & Featherman, 1983; Stedman, 1987):

- Reason for the parental separation (death, divorce, or desertion).
- Age of the child at the time of parental separation.
- Personal relationships in the one-parent household.

For similar reasons, much of the early research on the educational achievement of one-parent children is flawed. Most of the studies lumped all one-parent families together and failed to consider other potentially important factors, such as the existence of extended family or other social support systems. In addition, many studies selected participants who were referred to psychiatric clinics, a population not representative of single-parent families (Hammond, 1979). More recent studies of "normal" populations of single-parent families have concentrated on suburban, white, middle-class families, again not a reliable sample of one-parent families. Early databases that lacked adequate family background information also hampered the research. Fortunately some recent studies have been much more comprehensive.

Children's Adaptations to Divorce

Many researchers who have studied the effects of single-parent family life on children have limited their research to children of divorced families. Divorce is the most common way for children to enter one-parent families, and has been a topic of concern itself. Most divorce research has examined how children adapt to life in such families, and what factors influence the children's adjustment. How well a child handles life in a one-parent household is considered key to a child's functioning in other areas, such as school. When a child is under stress at home, his or her reactions often spill over into school activities. The Children of Single Parents and the Schools Project seeks to understand the reasons why children in one-parent families tend to fall behind their two-parent peers in school.

Divorce researchers have made several important findings concerning children's adaptation to life with one parent. First, studies have found a considerable variety in children's responses to divorce. A child's ability to cope with divorce depends in part on his or her age, past experience, and stage of development. Second, the research suggests that a child's adjustment to changes in his or her family's structure may be easier when the following conditions exist: both parents continue to maintain a close relationship with the child, there is little conflict between the two parents, the parents cooperate in consistent child-rearing, and other supports are consistently available to the family (*Single Parents . . . ,* 1983).

Great Diversity in Children's Responses. The initial research approach to single-parent families has been criticized for its negative focus on the problems caused by divorce. More recent research studies have found that not all children are adversely affected by divorce. Divorce can actually help children from two-parent families where there was high marital conflict prior to the divorce by ending or reducing the family's hostilities and uncertainties. A 1981 national study found that high levels of marital conflict in "intact" homes appeared to be as harmful as marital disruption itself (Peterson & Zill, 1986). In general, researchers confirm that children function better in one-parent or step-parent families than in conflict-ridden nuclear families (Hetherington, Hagan, & Anderson, in press). However, even when divorce is the best solution to a destructive family relationship, almost all children experience great pain during the divorce transition period.

For the most part, children of divorce are normal, healthy children who are confronted with an extremely stressful situation (Wilkinson, 1977). Although marital conflict and instability cause a variety of behavior problems and a need for psychological help in some children, most children of divorce do not need and do not get counseling, nor do they show especially high levels of behavior problems. It is when children are exposed to multiple "stressors" during divorce (parental conflict, reduced economic resources, changes in parental availability and parenting style, and chaotic household routines) that the adverse effects of divorce are multiplied (Wilkinson, 1977). In general, most children and parents can cope with and adapt to the short-term crisis of divorce within a two to three year period if their situation is not compounded by continued or additional adversity (Hetherington, Hagan, & Anderson, in press).

Children can exhibit problems at different times during this transition period, either just before the marital separation, or immediately following a parent's departure. Some children experience delayed stress reactions occurring years after the divorce, especially in adolescence (Hetherington, Hagan, & Anderson, in press). Many children show a remarkable ability to cope with the transition and in the long term may actually be enhanced by their handling of the change, while others suffer sustained developmental disruptions.

Most children manifest some problem behaviors and emotional upheaval immediately following their parents' divorce or remarriage. Children commonly feel angry, resentful, anxious, depressed, and even guilty. Some children react by withdrawing from the crisis, and become listless, quiet, or moody. Others react to the parental conflict by becoming disobedient, and by acting aggressively towards peers and adults (*Single Parents . . . ,* 1983). One landmark 1970's study of sixty suburban, middle-class families conducted by Judith Wallerstein and Joan Kelly detailed the psychological impact of divorce on children (Wallerstein & Kelly, 1980).

Wallerstein and Kelly Study. In their eight-year study, Wallerstein and Kelly interviewed 131 children between the ages of 3 and 18 whose parents were going through a divorce, and found certain common reactions among the children. They found that during divorce the children all experienced a greater sense of vulnerability and all worried who would take care of them in the future. About half of the children were afraid of being abandoned by their father, and one-third of the children feared that their mother might also desert them. Feeling dependent on one parent rather than on both parents together, the children often worried about the health and well-being of the remaining parent. In addition they wondered about each parent's ability to cope without the other's help.

Next, the children felt very burdened by their sadness over the loss of their original family unit. More then half of the children were openly tearful, moody, and sad. One-third showed symptoms of depression which included restlessness, difficulties with sleeping and concentrating, feelings of emptiness, play inhibition, compulsive overeating, and complaints of physical aches and pains. Two-thirds of the children, especially the youngest ones, longed for the absent parent and fantasized about their parents' reconciliation.

The children also experienced their parent's exit from the family home as an indication that the departing parent had lost interest in them. These children perceived their parents' preoccupation with their own problems as additional signs of rejection. Over half of the children, and especially the young boys, felt rejected by one or both parents during this time. The children became profoundly lonely as their fathers moved out of the house and their mothers went to work outside the home. Their loneliness was most acute when they waited many hours after school for their working parent to return home, or when they were home alone on weekends while their parents had other activities.

These children also experienced many inner conflicts about their parents' divorce. In over two-thirds of the families studied the parents openly competed for their children's affection and allegiance. Even when this did not occur the children felt a sense of divided loyalties. Many school-aged children saw themselves in the lonely position at the center of their parents' struggles. Far fewer of the children perceived themselves as the cause of their parents' divorce. Only one-third of the children, mainly those eight years old or younger, felt responsible in some way for their family's disruption and often attributed the parents' rift to something that they had done or had failed to do.

Finally, children and adolescents of all ages experienced a rise in aggression. The youngest children expressed their aggressive feelings through increased temper tantrums and hitting of other siblings, while older children took out their aggressions through direct expressions of anger and verbal attacks against others. Over one-third of the children, and especially older boys, experienced anger as a major component of the divorce (Wallerstein & Kelly, 1980).

Differences in Children's Reactions to Divorce

Children can "survive, win, or lose" in divorce situations depending on their personal characteristics, age, gender, available resources, subsequent life experiences, and personal relationships (Hetherington, in press). Some researchers argue that the ultimate outcome of divorce depends most on the nature and quality of a child's post-divorce living arrangements and on the complexity and duration of the changes that a child must go through during the divorce transition.

Personality. Divorce studies have found that a child's ability to handle his or her parents' divorce depends in part on the child's temperament and stage of development. "Difficult" children have been found to be more vulnerable to stress than "easy" children. For example, a child who has trouble adjusting to change and getting used to new situations or who is easily frightened and upset may have more post-divorce problems than a more carefree child. A child's intelligence, independence, sense of inner control, and self-esteem can also positively influence his/her adaptability to stressful life experiences (Hetherington, Hagan, & Anderson, in press).

Age. Although there have been few studies investigating the effect of children's ages on their ability to adjust to divorce, the consensus is that children of differing ages have different types of coping mechanisms and behavior problems (Hetherington, in press). Wallerstein and Kelly reported that the most striking response of children aged six to eight to their parents' separation was their pervasive sadness and their great difficulty in getting any relief from their sorrow (Hetherington, Camara, & Featherman, 1983). To these young children the stress and turmoil of divorce often seemed inescapable possibly because, unlike pre-school children, this age group did not use fantasy as a way to deny their loss.

Older school-age children aged nine to twelve were much more resourceful in their ability to cope with their profound feelings of loss and rejection. One of the focus group mothers told how her daughter took out all the public library's children's books on divorce when the parents separated. But these children often felt different from their peers, ashamed of what was happening in their families, and embarrassed by their parents' behavior. Adolescents aged thirteen to eighteen also experienced considerable pain and anger when their parents divorced. They would often take advantage of outside support systems in order to disengage themselves from their families, either constructively through friends and school activities, or destructively through anti-social activities (Wallerstein & Kelly, 1980).

Gender. Recent studies have modified the traditional wisdom that boys are more traumatized by divorce than girls. Newer studies have found that in mother-custody families, boys tend to have more difficulty than girls, exhibiting more impulsive, anti-social, and aggressive behavior and experiencing more interpersonal problems with parents, teachers, and peers. On the other hand, girls tend to react with lower self-esteem, anxiety, and depression (though the research findings are not consistent on this issue) (Hetherington, 1983). Wallerstein and Guidubaldi have found that at the outset of parents' divorce, boys of elementary school age seem to have more problems than girls, while girls tend to experience a delayed reaction, reacting most strongly to the divorce during their adolescence (Guidubaldi et al., 1986).

There are several theories about the differences in boys' and girls' adjustment to divorce. In part, boys may be exposed to more marital conflict than girls because parents may be more willing to fight in front of a boy rather than a girl, yet boys receive less outside support during the crisis from teachers and friends. Sex-role stereotypes might also influence boys' and girls' responses to divorce. Boys may be expected to control their feelings and to require less support than girls, but at the same time they may be permitted to display more disruptive behavior than girls (Hetherington, Camara, & Featherman, 1983).

One of the most important findings from studies concerning father-only families is that children tend to function better in the custody of the same-sex parent (Hetherington, in press). Studies have found that girls in father-only families tend to have the same behavior problems as boys who live with their mothers. The reasons for this are still unclear. Because most boys and girls remain with their mothers under current custody arrangements, boys may experience more post-divorce adjustment problems than girls for this reason.

Death vs. Divorce: A Child's View. A few researchers have looked at whether the death of a parent affects children in the same way that divorce can affect them. Some experts consider children whose parent has died to be better off, certainly financially but also emotionally, than children who have lost a father through desertion or divorce. As with divorce, however, much of a child's adaptation depends on the mother's ability to cope with the loss (Adams, 1984). A recent study found that in the long run, children do better when they are allowed to discuss the death openly and to express their emotions concerning the death.

An important difference between death and divorce for a child is that although death is final, divorce is never over. Because most children of divorce suffer a major separation from one parent, it might be expected that they go through a grieving period similar to that experienced by bereaved children. Some experts argue that indeed the grief process is quite similar in both cases. But the obvious distinction remains that after divorce a child still has the possibility of maintaining some relationship with both parents.

Children who experience the death of a parent tend to react by withdrawing and by showing heightened shyness and timidity (Burns, 1982). In contrast, children of divorce are apt to exhibit more aggressive, acting-out behavior. Very often a child whose parent has died does not know anyone else in the same situation and feels particularly isolated and "special" in a distressing way.

Influence of Parents on Children's Adjustment

The problems that a parent encounters adjusting to single-parent life can greatly influence the adjustment of his or her children. Some experts have argued that most of the differences observed in children from single-parent homes can be attributed to the increased social, emotional, and financial stresses experienced by the custodial parents (Devall, Soneman, & Brody, 1986). According to "family restructuring" theory, the three most important factors which influence the adjustments of parents to life in a one-parent household are (Ihinger-Tallman, 1986; Green, 1981; Phelps & Huntley, 1985):

- Parent's financial stability and security.
- Parent's capacity to learn new coping skills.
- Community resources and social supports available to the family.

Custodial Parent/Child Relationship. The capacity of the custodial parent to "cope" plays an important role in children's short-term adjustment to divorce (Burns & Brassard, 1982; Hetherington, Hagan, & Anderson, in press). Some researchers have concluded that a parent's economic resources (their educational level, annual income, etc.) may be the most important adjustment factor. Other researchers emphasize that a single parent's emotional health and ability to handle stress depend on the adequacy of his or her support networks (Phelps & Huntley, 1985; Gladow & Ray, 1986). Whatever the cause of a parent's emotional state, researchers point out that the children of depressed, anxious, or dissatisfied parents are more likely to feel rejected and unhappy. As family stress increases, regardless of its source, the parent's capacity for nurturing decreases (Schorr & Schorr, 1988).

Children tend to have fewer behavior problems after divorce when their custodial parent is able to provide a consistent, stable environment. Without daily love, discipline, and guidance, children are ill-prepared to cope with such major life changes as divorce. Children perform better at home and school when they have set routines, regular meals, and a organized home life (Appel, 1985).

Recently divorced custodial mothers are more likely to feel distressed than married mothers, becoming extremely preoccupied and emotionally unavailable to their children. It is not uncommon for custodial mothers to become self-involved, uncommunicative, non-supportive, and inconsistent in dealing with their children (Hetherington, Hagan, & Anderson, in press). This problem is compounded for employed mothers by their work hours outside the home. As a consequence of the parents' additional stresses, children often experience "diminished parenting" during this difficult post-divorce period (Appel, 1985). These mothers tend to become less supportive of their children's efforts to handle the routine challenges of friendships, school, homework, and family life.

In contrast to custodial mothers, there are very few studies of custodial fathers, partly due to the small numbers of custodial fathers and to researchers' delayed interest in this phenomenon. The studies that do exist show that, like custodial mothers, custodial fathers report difficulty in coping with the stresses of divorce, and may also exhibit "diminished parenting" soon after divorce. The limited studies available provide no evidence that custodial fathers are different from custodial mothers in their ability to raise children alone (Appel, 1985).

However, several recent studies do indicate that father-only families tend to function more effectively and experience fewer problems than those of mother-only families. But these comparisons between father-only and mother-only families may reflect other non-parenting differences between the two groups. Single fathers may have an easier time raising their children because these fathers are more likely to have older children, to be financially well-off, and to actively seek custody of the children (rather than merely assenting to it). In addition, non-custodial mothers are more likely than non-custodial fathers to maintain contact with their children, which may also influence the quality of the custodial parent/child relationship (Hetherington, in press).

Non-custodial Parent/Child Relationship. Research has found that, regardless of a child's family structure, both parents remain vitally important to the child. The part that the non-custodial parents play in their children's lives is crucial to the children's post-divorce adjustment. Children who have close relationships with both parents after divorce (provided that the relationships are not destructive ones) tend to have far fewer behavioral problems, troubles with peers, or academic difficulties than children who have a good post-divorce relationship with only one or neither parent. Parenting support from non-custodial fathers is found to be an especially important factor in the post-divorce adjustment of boys (Guidubaldi, 1986).

Despite the fact that the presence of the non-custodial parent is so critical after divorce, within two years of the family transition the typical non-custodial parent—90 percent of whom are fathers—has usually withdrawn from his family both in terms of child-rearing and child support (Hetherington, in press). Post-divorce fathers are more likely to visit and to pay child support for sons than for daughters (Hetherington, Camara, Featherman, 1983).

In the early 1980's a national study, the National Survey of Children, of 1,400 children between the ages of 12 and 16 found that, within a few years of divorce, the majority of non-custodial fathers had no regular contact with their children and provided little or no financial support. In this study, 52 percent of all the adolescents living with separated, divorced, or remarried mothers had not seen their fathers in more than a year and 35 percent of the children had not seen their fathers in the past five years. Only 16 percent saw their fathers as often as once a week (Zill & Rogers, 1988). These absent fathers were not compensating for the lack of personal contact by writing letters or making telephone calls to their children (Peterson, 1986). The vast majority of the children in the study had virtually lost their non-custodial fathers.

Parental Cooperation. Those non-custodial parents who maintain contact with their children rarely play more than a minor parenting role in rearing of their children. The relationship between a child and the outside parent is usually a social exchange in which the adult acts more like a friend than a parent (Furstenberg & Nord, 1985). And the non-custodial parent is more likely to have a relationship with his children than with his ex-spouse (Zill & Rogers, 1988). Most divorced parents engage in "parallel parenting" rather than in cooperative parenting and have very little direct communication with each other (Peterson, 1986). A child adjusts better to situations of low post-divorce conflict when the parents agree to use cooperative, consistent child-rearing practices. Some proponents of shared custody arrangements argue that joint custody awards ease tensions and increase cooperation between divorcing parents. However, successful cooperative shared custody situations seem to be fairly rare.

Educational Achievement of One-Parent Children

Studies comparing the school records of children from one-parent and two-parent families have found that children raised in one-parent homes have an increased risk of poor academic achievement (Burns & Brassard, 1982). Life in a one-parent family seems to affect a child's school performance adversely (as measured by test scores, grades, and conduct reports) as well as their total educational attainment (as measured by the number of years of education completed, high school drop-out rates, and successful completion of college) (*Single Parents . . . ,* 1983). The consensus is that relatively little of the harm is directly caused by the absence of one parent. Instead, much more of the problem is associated with the family's lack of income and related stresses that typically accompany a parent's absence (Stedman, 1987).

Many analysts conclude that after family background and income level differences between one-parent and two-parent families are taken into account, life with one parent lowers a child's academic achievement to a relatively small though real extent. Others argue that this direct effect is so small as to be unimportant, and that the low income level of single-parent families accounts for nearly all of the total harm associated with one-parent status (Blechman, 1982). Recent studies suggest that family member attitudes towards education and the ways in which family members relate to each other in a single-parent household have greater impact on a child's achievement than do family background characteristics (education levels, etc.) (Henderson, 1986; Linney & Vemberg, 1983). In the next sections we will explore in more detail how living in a one-parent household can affect a child's life in school, and what circumstances allow children from single-parent homes to succeed academically.

Academic Performance Gap. Research studies have compared the school performances of one-parent and two-parent children in a number of ways. Most studies compared scores from intelligence (IQ) tests and aptitude tests such as the Scholastic Aptitude Test (SAT) which are often used to predict children's future achievement. After reviewing thirty such studies, Hetherington, Camara, and Featherman reported that overall the studies found one-parent children academically behind two-parent children, with nineteen of the thirty studies recording lower scores for children from one-parent homes (Hetherington, Camara, & Featherman, 1983). The differences found in these studies were usually small, an average of three to four points less for one-parent children. Several of the studies noted that these small differences decreased when children of similar socioeconomic status were compared.

Hetherington and her colleagues also reviewed the results of eleven studies that compared the scores of standardized achievement tests measuring students' verbal and quantitative skills. In seven of the eleven studies, one-parent children received lower scores than children from two-parent families, with the differences between the two student groups averaging less than one school year. A 1986 study by Milne and her associates similarly reported lower reading and math achievement scores for one-parent children (Milne, Myers, & Rosenthal, 1986). The differences in scores were significantly reduced when these studies took into account (controlled for) the socioeconomic differences between the one-parent and two-parent students (Hetherington, Camara, & Featherman, 1983).

Teacher-assigned grades and grade-point averages (GPAs) are other important indicators of academic performance. Grades test how well students meet specific objectives set by their teachers and reflect a student's ability to adapt his or her behavior to the teacher's expectations. Grades are considered better predictors of success in college than college entrance exams. Hetherington's review found that in studies which adequately controlled for economic differences in the children's family backgrounds, students in one-parent homes received substantially lower grades than two-parent children (Hetherington, Camara, & Featherman, 1983). The differences found in the children's grades were larger than the differences found in the children's more objective test scores (Garfinkel & McLanahan, 1986). The implication of the wider gap between one-parent and two-parent children's grades is that teachers may grade one-parent children below their objective performance levels. This is an important issue which will be discussed in more detail later in this chapter.

Educational Attainment. Completed years of schooling is another important indicator of academic achievement. A number of studies have confirmed that children who spend even a short time in a one-parent family complete fewer years of school on average than children in two-parent families, even when family background factors such as family income, ethnicity, and parent's education are taken into account. These are significant research results because educational attainment is a key predictor of later economic well-being. Most of these studies used only boys as subjects, and so the research results may not necessarily hold true for girls. Here are some of these studies' findings:

Featherman and Hauser's 1978 study found that males raised in a one-parent family completed about three-quarters of a year less schooling than males raised in two-parent households. A decade later Krein's study found that the proportion of young men from one-parent families who fail to finish high school is twice the proportion among those who have always lived in a two-parent family. In addition, males from two-parent families are twice as likely to finish college as males from one-parent families (Krein, 1986). A study by Krein and Beller also reported that living in a one-parent family reduces the educational attainment of sons by half a school year and of daughters about one-fifth of a school year.

Causes of Lower Scholastic Achievement

Why do children from single-parent homes receive lower grades than children who have two parents at home? What causes the greater disparity in the students' grades than in their standardized test scores?

Behavior Problems. One explanation is that children from one-parent families have more difficulty adapting their behavior to teacher expectations than two-parent children. In Wallerstein and Kelly's study, teachers reported negative behavior changes in two-thirds of the children after divorce, changes which included increased restlessness, daydreaming, sadness, difficulty concentrating on schoolwork, and an exaggerated need for the teacher's attention (Goldstein, 1985).

Also, after divorce many children experience unexpected mood changes and outbursts of anger and irritation while at school. Hetherington's research review noted that children in divorced families tend to be more disruptive in class, to have less efficient study habits, and to be tardy or absent more often than two-parent children (Hetherington, Camara, & Featherman, 1983). Some studies report that children in one-parent families have more household chores than children in two-parent families (Amato, 1987). These additional duties may reduce the time these children have for completing their homework.

Less Motivation. The behaviors described above can affect a child's school performance in several different ways. These behaviors may be interfering with the child's ability to concentrate and learn, as shown by poor quality classroom work and incomplete homework assignments (Hetherington, Camara, & Featherman, 1983). Another theory is that a child from a one-parent family is more likely to underachieve because the stresses associated with major family transitions may lower the child's self-determination and motivation to do well in school. But the teacher may also influence a child's self-perceptions and behavior by expecting less from the child because he or she is from a one-parent family.

Teacher Attitude. A third explanation is that teachers may perceive children who do not conform to school routines and requirements as less competent, regardless of the

children's intellectual ability. In addition, teachers may have
other negative attitudes regarding single-parent children. Research studies have found that teachers may sometimes antic-
ipate negative behavior from one-parent children and respond to their behavior problems in overly negative ways
(Stedman, 1987; Santrock & Russel, 1978).

Fewer Family Resources. Researchers theorize that
children from one-parent families complete less schooling
because single parents have fewer personal and financial resources to invest in their children's education (Milne, Myers,
& Rosenthal, 1986). According to this "household production" theory, a child's educational attainment is seen as a
product of the parents' personal time and money "inputs."
Time and money are typically more limited in one-parent
than in two-parent homes.

Low family income in particular affects a child's education in a myriad of ways. Poor families have less money to
invest in educational material and activities for their children.
Such educational "investments" may include purchases of
children's books, high quality educationally oriented child
care, extra-curricular activities, private tutoring sessions, vacations involving travel, and summer camp opportunities. In
a study of low-income divorced women, the mothers reported being forced to cut down on such essentials as their
children's school lunches and school supplies in addition to
limiting their children's after-school activities (Weitzman,
1985).

Older children in low-income single-parent families
sometimes work in after-school jobs as delivery workers,
baby-sitters, or store clerks in order to supplement their family's income. These part-time jobs necessarily leave less time
for homework. Many single-parent children may also quit
high school early in order to earn money for their families, or
conversely, to leave a stressful family situation. Low income is
also associated with family instability and stress; poor families
tend to suffer from unemployment and to live in unsafe neighborhoods where there are high delinquency rates and poor
quality schools (Garfinkel & McLanahan, 1986; McLanahan,
1986).

Time is also a scarce resource in one-parent homes. Single parents who work full-time have less time to spend with their children: talking with them and meeting their emotional needs, helping them with their homework assignments, reading stories to them, and taking them to museums. These parents also have little time for other school-related activities such as parent/teacher conferences, school assemblies, PTA meetings, and volunteering for school trips or class activities. These kinds of parent involvement activities are thought to help children's performance in schools significantly, though few studies have looked at the specific effects of the forms and levels of parent-school involvement (Linney & Vemberg, 1983).

Some recent studies have found that single working mothers do not spend less time with their children than do married working mothers (Amato, 1987). Instead, single mothers tend to compensate by spending the least time of all mothers on household chores, volunteer activities, and on personal care (e.g., personal grooming, resting, sleeping, and eating) (Sanik & Maudlin, 1986). The single working mother's sacrifice of personal time, however, can gradually increase her stress level over time and thus can still adversely affect her children.

Household production theory counts parental time in terms of parents' time spent per day on educational activities as well as the total amount of time that a child spends in a one-parent family. According to this theory, parents spend the greatest amount of time that parents spend with their children per day on developmentally important activities during the pre-school years. After that, school staff and peers supplement the parents' role in working with children on school-related activities. In support of this theory, Wallerstein and Kelly found that in the short run, pre-schoolers are most affected developmentally by their parents' divorce (Krein, 1988).

In the long run, Krein argues, the children who are most harmed academically are those who have lived the longest time in a one-parent family, i.e., children who were young when their parents separated. Krein and Beller's recent study confirms that the total length of time that a child spends in a one-parent home correlates negatively with the child's total number of years spent in school (Krein, 1988).

Positive Influences on Academic Achievement

What improves the school achievement of one-parent children? Researchers think that certain family processes can help a child's school achievement more than the mere fact of having two parents at home (Linney & Vemberg, 1983). Parents' expectations for good school performance are very powerful influences on a child's behavior. Milne's study, for example, found that for both black and white children, parents' academic expectations significantly tempered the effect of living with one parent (Milne, Myers, & Rosenthal, 1986). Clark also has found that in both poor and middle-class families, children who do well in school have one or two parents who:

- clearly value school.
- have a sense of self-mastery over their lives.
- give the children positive reinforcement about their schoolwork.
- provide an organized home with regular routines and meal times.
- encourage their children to make good use of their time.

Overall, children seem to adapt best, learn most, and misbehave least when home and school are both organized, predictable settings that are responsive to and nurturing of the children's needs.

The research summarized here points out the dangers of stereotyping children from one-parent families as poor students. Many other factors, including the stability and consistency of the child's family life and the child's continuing relationships with both of his or her parents, are also important predictor's of the child's academic success. Yet the research also identifies the underlying conditions, often present in one-parent families, that can put children at risk for academic failure. Children in the midst of acrimonious divorces, grieving over the loss of a parent, or living in emotionally stressed and financially strapped households are vulnerable to trouble in school, and possibly to educational disaster. The next chapter will discuss in more detail the treatment one-parent children receive at school.

Chapter Four:

SCHOOL LIFE FOR ONE-PARENT CHILDREN

American elementary schools serve relatively few families who match the familiar "Leave It to Beaver" image. In 1987, the once "typical" American family—husband as earner, wife as homemaker, and two children—accounted for only 3.7 percent (2.4 million) of the nation's families (U.S. Department of Labor, 1987). The change in profile of American families carries profound implications for this country's schools. Just as today's one-parent families don't resemble the families typical of past decades, the educational requirements of one-parent children don't match the educational needs of children from traditional two-parent families. In the next two chapters we will examine the school needs of one-parent families and the adaptations elementary schools have made to meet the needs of this new school population.

High Quality Education

On a basic level, children from one-parent families need the same high quality education that children of two-parent families expect: schools that offer positive learning environments in which children can perform at their full potential. Researchers have found that effective schools share certain organizational and philosophical characteristics. These educational similarities include (Schorr & Schorr, 1988):

- An emphasis on academics.
- A safe, orderly, disciplined environment.
- A school principal who takes vigorous, instructional leadership.

- Teachers who have high expectations that all students can and will learn.
- Regular and frequent reviews of a child's progress with the child's family.
- Agreement among parents and school staff on the school's goals.

Many one-parent children who live in comfortable or affluent communities have access to schools which possess these educational characteristics. The children in these neighborhoods have plenty of opportunity to succeed in school, provided that their individual needs for assistance are met.

But millions of one-parent children currently live in poverty, many of them residing in disadvantaged areas where schools are hard pressed to offer the educational environment necessary to prepare students for future success. Education has traditionally provided an escape for children from poor families, yet in many predominantly poor, minority school districts, the drop-out rates range from 30 to 50 percent. In some inner-city schools, drop-out rates exceed 80 percent (Committee for Economic Development, 1987). These schools often alienate rather than educate their disadvantaged students, many of whom come from one-parent families.

One-parent children can suffer from discouraging school environments as much if not more than other groups of students. The extra attention and personal support that one-parent children may need to stay on track in school is often missing from overburdened schools. In the summer of 1988 we interviewed teachers and single parents from tough, urban schools which serve primarily one-parent children. These parents and teachers had similar ideas about the ways in which schools could pay more attention to their students. Their school improvement suggestions included: decreasing class size so that teachers can relate to fewer students; employing high school students, parents, and senior citizens as teacher aides or monitors to provide extra care and support to students needing extra help; and increasing teachers' salaries to provide incentives for good teachers to remain in the public school system. We received comparable recommendations from the research literature and from education experts (Kennedy, Jung, & Orland, 1986). Although these approaches are not specifically targeted to one-parent children, many one-parent children could undoubtedly benefit from the extra attention of caring adults.

The problems of the schools that serve America's poorest children are of great concern, although a complete analysis of the problems and potential solutions for these schools lies beyond the scope of this discussion. Instead, this chapter will focus on two educational needs which are specific to one-parent children. First, all one-parent students require respect for their family status from their teachers and school administrators. Students have trouble when they don't feel accepted at school. Second, some one-parent children face periods of family crisis (such as death, separation, or divorce), during which they require special support and assistance at school. We will discuss these issues of prejudice and crisis support below.

School Attitudes Toward One-Parent Children

Stigma Against Single Parents. Children from one-parent families require the same respect that two-parent children receive from school personnel. However, research to date reveals that school teachers, administrators, and staff too often stereotype one-parent children as victims of "broken" homes, an attitude which assumes that one-parent families are abnormal and dysfunctional (Rich, 1988). Through a research review, followed by focus group interviews with single mothers, one-parent children, and teachers, we found that, in general, one-parent families get a very mixed reception from schools. While the teachers and administrators in some schools show great sensitivity to the concerns and feelings of one-parent students, in other schools many personnel maintain negative attitudes and expectations about children who do not come from "intact families."

The terms "broken home" and "intact family" reveal the social stigma that one-parent families endure. In the past, an illegitimate birth or a divorce in the family was considered a

shameful family secret. "Bastard" children and their mothers were often ostracized by their communities. To some extent these negative social attitudes continue to exist. Researcher Judith Worell points out, "Given the incidence of single-parent homes, it seems curious that these families are frequently regarded as deviant or unhealthy, and that considerable stigma is still attached to the status of the single mother" (Worell, 1986). In a 1984 study of sixty divorced mothers, a majority of the women complained about the social stigma associated with single parenting (Arendell, 1984). Many of these women said they felt that society expected their children to be candidates for delinquency and other abnormal behaviors simply because they were raised by a divorced mother.

In many schools the attitudes of teachers, administrators, and staff about students from single-parent families reflect this social prejudice. In a 1981 national survey of 1,200 single parents from 47 states conducted by the National Committee for Citizens in Education, 62 percent of the parents surveyed thought that school personnel did not see the single-parent family as a "normal" family. Forty-five percent of the parents reported that the school assumes that any problems their children have are caused by their single-parent status (*Single Parents . . .*, 1983). Barry Knight, author of a Parents Without Partners guide for single parents, asserted that "schools are sometimes the worst offenders against single parents" (Knight, 1980).

We found from our focus group interviews with single mothers that while many of the mothers had positive interactions with some teachers, the mothers also thought that other teachers and administrators were insensitive and unsympathetic to the needs of one-parent families. As one divorced mother stated:

> Schools should give a positive image that this is a single woman, working hard, overcoming insurmountable problems, incredible stress, [who] has made it and should feel very proud. Instead of that image, it's "You failed at a marriage." It's the traditional view. They don't give you the credit as females, as heads of households, for what you have accomplished. That image should be put forth.

The group of never-married mothers we interviewed felt that among all single-parent families, they and their children had particular difficulties with school personnel. Two of these mothers reported feeling quite patronized by school teachers and administrators. A third mother observed:

> I think a lot of this bottom-lines to sex and to the fact that we've had sex and we've had children without being married. I think that a lot of people are extremely uncomfortable with that and it's very difficult for people to face it with the child every day.

The remarks made by the focus group of elementary school teachers tended to confirm the comments from some of the never-married mothers. For example, when asked what differences, if any, the teachers found among children from various types of one-parent families, one teacher replied, "The child of a never-married mother is like a child with a limb missing. They get used to it and compensate for it." This teacher considered such children maimed by their family status, a terribly negative view of children from never-married families. In the next sections we will outline what impact such teacher attitudes can have on the education of one-parent children.

Teacher/Student Relationships. Undeniably, the most important person at school for a child is his or her teacher. For many students, especially those from one-parent families, their teacher becomes their parent away from home. In the classroom, teachers can be a great help to children who need individual academic assistance or who may need some personal time and attention to cope with a family crisis. Classroom teachers are often the most stable elements in the life of a child whose parents are in the midst of a separation or divorce. In a family where a child has little or no contact with his or her non-custodial parent, the establishment in school of a good relationship with an adult, especially an adult of the same sex as the absent parent, may particularly help the child. If a teacher has a continuing relationship with a student during a family transition, he or she can quickly identify any new problems, provide immediate support to the student, and arrange prompt referrals for more intensive help, if necessary (Drake, 1981).

Unfortunately, many school teachers and administrators stereotype children from single-parent families as problem students. Researchers have found a consistent teacher bias against children from one-parent households (Linney & Vemberg, 1983). School personnel tend to expect more behavior problems and lower academic performance from these children than from children in two-parent families (Rich, 1988). Researchers Carol Will and Mary Lou Fuller argue that teachers also tend to fixate on crisis-related behavior problems and to assume incorrectly that all single-parent children are in the midst of some family-related crisis. In the 1981 National Committee of Citizens for Education survey of single parents, many parents reported hearing school personnel express surprise that their children had adjusted so well to life after divorce (Clay, 1981).

Teachers' expectations concerning one-parent children strongly influence the teachers' actions, attitudes, and classroom teaching behaviors concerning these children (Linney & Vemberg, 1983). Research findings suggest that teachers' expectations color their subjective assessments of student performance (including report card grades), and that teachers appear to base their judgments of students on their observations of the students' family background (Blechman, 1982). The significant discrepancies that researchers have found between the scores of objective performance measures (IQ tests) and subjective measures (school grades) of students from one-parent families may partly result from teachers' negative expectations for these students. In addition, teacher expectations may also influence the students' actual performance by influencing the students' own perceptions of their abilities (Hammond, 1979).

Children's Self-Perceptions. Many children from single-parent families already feel somewhat isolated and different from other children because of their family status. They are often not encouraged to talk about their family situation with friends, teachers, or other adults, and so their feelings of being atypical remain (Burns & Brassard, 1982). In interviews with researcher Jill Krementz, several children of deceased parents said they were worried that people would treat them differently at school after their parent died. These children felt that no one would "treat them like normal," that people would consider them helpless or feel sorry for them, and would not talk with them or want to play with them (Krementz, 1981).

In our focus group interviews with elementary school children, several children of separated or divorced parents also described feeling different from their classmates and somewhat alone at school because of their family status. According to one never-married mother interviewed, her daughter believes she is the only child in her particular family situation in her entire elementary school. This mother commented, "They [one-parent children] bear this tremendous burden that they are different." The elementary teachers we interviewed thought their single-parent students often felt hurt by not having a "mom and dad" like their friends. One teacher concluded, "They feel left out."

Studies have also found that single-parent children often perceive themselves as doing worse than their two-parent classmates in a variety of ways. One study of 420 "intact" family children and 63 children from divorced or separated homes indicated that the single-parent children saw themselves as having less appropriate and more negative behavior than two-parent children in three areas—at home, in school, and in their interpersonal relationships (Delaney, Richards, & Strathe, 1984). In this study the teachers rated the divorced/separated children's school behavior higher than these children rated themselves. In another study, the children from divorced families did not have greater responsibilities or engage in fewer activities than other children, but still perceived themselves as less involved than two-parent children, reporting fewer visits with friends and lower social competency than children from two-parent families (Devall, Soneman, & Brody, 1986).

Any additional negative messages and insensitive treatment tend to reinforce these students' poor self-images and increase their perceptions that they are not "normal." For this reason all school staff, especially teachers, must guard against negative assumptions that one-parent children come from "broken," dysfunctional families. School personnel need to understand that many one-parent children do not have academic and behavioral problems, but that some one-parent children do need additional attention or assistance because of their family situation (Hammond, 1979).

School Policies for One-Parent Families

School Notification. Teachers and other school personnel can help a one-parent child only if the school is aware of the child's family situation. According to the 1981 National Committee for Citizens in Education survey, 80 percent of the single parents polled said that school personnel should know the parents' marital status in order to relate to the child as an individual and be responsive to the child's particular needs (*Single Parents* . . . , 1983). Several single-parent family guides for schools have recommended that schools re-examine their student information practices for acquiring accurate family-status information. In such reviews schools should consider whether their student forms allow enough space for information about the student's non-custodial parent or step-family, how often the student information cards are updated, and how the information, especially concerning changes in family status and child custody, gets to teachers, counselors, and other school staff (Diamond, 1985).

Many parents hesitate to reveal this personal information about their single-parent status for fear that the knowledge might be abused by insensitive staff. While the single mothers in the focus groups felt that there were often good reasons for teachers to know that their children came from one-parent families, they expressed reservations about how the information might be used. One never-married mother cited an example in which she felt that the school had misused its knowledge about her dyslexic daughter's family status. The mother said, "The school tried to tell me that the reason she's dyslexic and reversed her b's and d's is because of her emotional condition, meaning she has no father." These mothers wanted the school staff to understand the child's situation, but not to use it as an instrument of blame.

Curriculum Issues. School curriculum materials are another means through which schools convey messages to students about the worth of their families. Research on classroom textbooks is based on the premise that the models of family life presented in these texts communicate social values to children and affect their attitude towards and acceptance of their own family situations (Conway & Mechler, 1983). Researchers argue that it is important that stories portray family life in a realistic way because children who cannot find their own families in their textbooks may feel bad about themselves and their families (Britton, Lumpkin, & Britton, 1984). According to Joan Kelly and Judith Wallerstein, the devotion of curriculum materials to the two-parent family "contributes to a greater sense of aloneness and difference in many one-parent children" (Conway & Mechler, 1983).

Past studies have focused on basal readers, such as the classic "Dick and Jane" series, because these textbooks are used for reading instruction in 90 percent of the elementary classrooms in the United States (Conway & Mechler, 1983; Britton, Lumpkin, & Britton, 1984). Analyses of American basal readers reveal that one-parent families are severely under-represented in stories. An early 1980's study of six basal readers series by Gwenyth Britton and her colleagues found that stories about one-parent families were vastly under-represented, shown in only 22 out of a total of 2,972 stories, less than one percent of all the readers' stories (Britton, Lumpkin, & Britton, 1984).

Another early 1980's study of eight basal reader series found that among the thousands of pieces there were 462 stories specifically about families. Nineteen percent of these 462 family-related stories portrayed one-parent families, 10 percent headed by women and 9 percent headed by men (Conway & Mechler, 1983). These readers misleadingly represented single mothers and single fathers in equal numbers, when in reality most single-parent families are headed by women. This study also reported that the subject of divorce was mentioned only three times in the 462 stories, and the death of a parent was mentioned only once.

We asked the teachers, mothers, and children in the summer focus groups what kinds of families they see represented in the classroom curriculum materials. The consensus among these groups was that the classroom textbooks currently in use do not reflect the great numbers of single-parent families in society. Several parents and teachers noted that there is popular literature about single-parent families available through public libraries and book distribution clubs such as Scholastic Books, but such literature is rarely used in the classroom. One parent said that when she offered some stories about homeless single-parent children to her son's teacher, the teacher declined to use the books, stating that the stories might bother her students. This reluctance to incorporate stories about one-parent family life into the classroom denies one-parent children an opportunity to feel more "at home" with their situation.

Classroom Activities. One of the focus group teachers pointed out that "the task of explaining to a child that what they have at home is acceptable is mainly taken up in classroom discussions." Some of the teachers described using family holidays such as Mother's Day and Father's Day to initiate class discussions about the variety of family types that exist, and to correct some students' derogatory attitudes about one-parent families. One teacher, whose kindergarten class was almost entirely filled with one-parent children (ten of whom were living with their grandmothers) admitted that she "tended to forget Father's Day." Some of the single mothers we interviewed mentioned handling these holidays by having their children make cards for other significant males, their uncles or grandfathers.

Two of the teachers interviewed during the focus group sessions enthusiastically described a new family life curriculum, recently approved for elementary schools throughout New York City, which includes the topic of single-parent families. The teachers viewed these new curriculum materials as a good opportunity to enlarge the discussion of families to include one-parent families. Researchers agree that school actions which expand the definition of the family in curriculum materials and which eliminate negative terminology and behavior in the classroom make the school atmosphere more comfortable and accepting for children from one-parent families (Elmore, 1986). In general, classroom teaching that ac-

knowledges the many variations of family life that exist—
including mother-headed, father-headed, grandmother-head-
ed, remarried, and joint custody families—make children
feel more secure in their particular family situation.

Many schools have become more sensitive to the concerns of their single-parent pupils. For example, on Father's
Day teachers at these schools do not ask children to honor
fathers with whom the children have had little or no contact.
Fewer schools also hold mother/daughter banquets or fa-
ther/son nights, or send notices home addressed to both parents. A 1986 report by the National Committee for Citizens
in Education summarized schools' progress in this area by
stating that "slowly, textbooks, curricula, school policy, and
teacher practices are becoming more sensitive to the fact that
many children—sometimes the majority—are not living with
both of their parents" (Henderson, et al., 1986). It is unfortu-
nate that no new national surveys have been conducted to
determine the current attitudes and practices of schools concerning single-parent families. Such a survey would be an
important step in documenting schools' progress on one-parent family issues.

Children in Family Crisis

Some children who are going through a family crisis
experience problems at school and do need some additional
support and attention in order to cope and adjust. Child
psychologists concur that it is unreasonable to assume that
children can function academically with no change in con-
centration, attention, interest level, and desire to learn at a
time when their family is in crisis. According to researcher
Arnold Stolberg, many teachers are faced with handling the
classroom consequences of divorce: dealing with unfinished
homework and with distracted, disruptive, and disrupted
students.

How Schools Can Help. What do children need during
crisis periods? Researchers agree on how teachers can help
their students make a successful transition through a family
crisis. They recommend that in these situations a teacher

should consider the following guidelines (Randall, 1981; Appel, 1985; Beckwith, Miller, Morris, & Sage, 1986; Diamond, 1985; Hetherington, Hagan, & Anderson, in press):

- Be understanding, warm, caring, and patient with the child.
- Acknowledge and actively listen to the child's feelings.
- Communicate with the child's family, and be available as a source of support for the child's family.
- Identify potential learning and behavior problems, and deal with them as soon as possible.
- Maintain high expectations for the child, and help validate and build the child's self-esteem.
- Monitor changes in the child's family status.

Other school personnel can also offer support to children under stress. Some elementary schools employ guidance counselors who can develop a good relationship with the students and their parents. In our focus group interviews the mothers warned that their children were reluctant to confide in their counselors because counselor assignments changed too frequently, and the counselors were too busy to meet with them. But education experts argue that school personnel can offer timely assistance if they are sensitive to children's situations.

Education expert Sara Lightfoot describes the John F. Kennedy High School, a large urban public school in the Bronx, that has an attendance/guidance department able to cut through academic red tape to help students through family crises. In this school, counselors take the time to listen to the students, focus on their personal situations, and respect their difficulties (Lightfoot, 1983). High school counselor Susan Diamond describes the extra attention and understanding that a school nurse can offer to children who are experiencing physical symptoms under the stress of a separation or divorce (Diamond, 1985). School principal John Ourth also writes about the assistance an elementary school principal can offer by talking with children and contacting their parents in special circumstances.

Overall, schools can be important supports to single-parent children during these crisis periods. Authoritative schools that provide warm, structured, and predictable environments can offer stability to children who face a period of "diminished parenting" and upheavals in family routines during a divorce (Hetherington, Hagan, & Anderson, in press). Studies confirm that schools with explicitly defined schedules, rules, and regulations; consistent, warm discipline; and expectations for mature behavior enhance the development of young children from divorced families (Schorr & Schorr, 1988). The "protective" effect of an authoritative school is most marked for boys, children with difficult temperaments, and children exposed to multiple life stresses (Hetherington, in press).

Teacher Training Programs. Many educators recommend that schools help single-parent children by changing the knowledge levels, attitudes, and educational approaches of those who must deal with them at school—their teachers and other school professionals (Randall, 1981). Often, schools bring in outside professionals to provide in-service training programs that instruct school staff about the needs of single-parent students and that sensitize staff to negative stereotypes they might have about these children (Drake, 1981).

Some experts suggest that teachers ought to receive training in the changing demographics of American school students and family-related child development issues as part of their teaching certification process. Other experts request that beginning teachers get help learning how to teach children from varied ethnic and socioeconomic backgrounds. Economic class differences may be the greatest barrier between some of these teachers and their one-parent students. New teachers could also be helped with including lessons about family structures, family transitions, and coping with family change into their classroom teaching. These family issues units could prepare children for the family changes that many of them are likely to go through by the time they leave high school. While some schools currently have informal in-service seminars for staff concerning one-parent families and consider such programs useful, to date no training packages or programs have been tested for their impact on the education of one-parent students.

School-Based Counseling. During periods of family trauma, schools can also provide special counseling services to help students adjust. Although most educators believe that the school's role is primarily to educate students and not to intervene in family matters, many education experts argue that the school also has a responsibility to help the child deal with and overcome emotional obstacles that might prevent the student from learning (Wilkinson & Blek, 1977). The two school services most often recommended for children who are adjusting to a death, divorce, or parental separation are individual counseling sessions with school psychologists, and children's support groups run by school guidance counselors or specifically trained teachers.

For several reasons, schools provide the most logical and readily available settings in which to offer children counseling services (Sumrak, 1984; Drake, 1981). For elementary school-age children, school is their major place of activity, a "second home" where it is natural for a child to turn for support. When group counseling is offered in schools, children can continue contact with others they meet in their group and they have the opportunity to establish some rapport with the school professional who leads the group (Moore, 1985). At a time when many parents are distracted by their own problems, alert teachers and staff can spot a child in trouble quickly, and can start counseling them early enough to prevent significant emotional damage and alleviate a need for later remedial help. It is important to note that when special counseling is offered in the school setting, parents and children do not have to contend with the cost, inconvenience, and possible stigma associated with using outside mental health services (Drake, 1981).

Although school guidance counselors and school psychologists can do some limited individual counseling with students, researchers have found group counseling in the form of children's support groups to be a more cost-effective way to help large numbers of students going through family crises like divorce (Gwynn & Brantley, 1987). A whole array of support group models have been developed, including one-day workshops for older children, transition groups that primarily provide emotional support for children, more structured groups that teach coping skills to children, and groups that combine the emotional support and coping skills components (Burns & Brassard, 1982). Some support groups, such as Liz McGonagle's "Banana Splits" program in Ballston Spa, New York, are fairly informal "rap" groups where children participate when they feel the need to talk about their troubles at home or with their peers. Other school-based programs are time-limited, closed membership groups run by one or two school professionals for up to eight students that meet during the school day once a week for ten to sixteen weeks.

Children's Support Groups. Today these school-based support groups are operating in schools throughout the country. According to the education specialists who created several of these group models, American school systems have purchased thousands of support group instruction manuals and workbooks in recent years. It is difficult to estimate the total number of existing groups, though the specialists interviewed thought that such groups are still not standard in school. Among the mothers we interviewed, one reported that her daughter attends such a children's support group in her New York City public elementary school. Two of the teachers we interviewed mentioned running such groups themselves.

For many schools, children's support groups are the main if not the only school service for one-parent children. Paul Ciborowski, a Sachem, Long Island high school guidance counselor and creator of a support group program, thinks that for many schools these support groups have practical appeal. These support groups are "add-on" programs run by counselors or teachers already on school staff, they are paid from counseling accounts already part of many schools' budgets, and they resemble school-based counseling groups for other school-related problems such as teen-age pregnancy, delinquency, and drug abuse, which are already in place in many schools.

Effective Programs. Are children's support group programs effective in providing help and support to single-parent children in distress? This project found no studies comparing individual vs. group counseling in schools, and found only a handful of studies which tested support group program models for their effects on program participants (Goldstein, 1985). Three academic researchers who have evaluated their support group model programs are JoAnne Pedro-Carroll who has a program in the Rochester, New York school system, Arnold Stolberg who runs a program in the Richmond, Virginia school system, and Judith Wallerstein who directs a program in the Corte Madera, California school system. These researchers have evaluated their divorce support groups and found them quite successful in helping children cope with and adjust to divorce (Gwynn & Brantley, 1987).

The groups conducted in these school districts share similar goals. Stolberg's program is designed to promote "academic, social, and emotional adjustment and the mastery of developmental tasks frequently hindered by divorce" (Stolberg, 1988). Pedro-Carroll's program is also intended to prevent or reduce the severity of the negative psychological consequences often associated with divorce. To achieve these goals the programs use similar methods. First, groups are designed to provide a supportive atmosphere where children can reduce their anxiety and stress by sharing their common feelings and concerns. Second, the groups teach the participants to develop problem-solving strategies and anger and communication skills that help them handle their family situations better.

There are also some differences among the group models. Pedro-Carroll's model incorporates many experiential exercises in addition to group discussions (a board game, film strips, role plays, etc.) and focuses on the children's emotional issues such as clarifying the children's misconceptions about divorce and their responsibility for parental conflict (Pedro-Carroll & Cowan, 1985). Stolberg's model puts more emphasis on cognitive learning; the group leaders teach coping skills through group projects and weekly assignments in a workbook completed by the children with the assistance of their parents. Stolberg also runs three evening sessions for the children's parents, designed to increase communication between the parents and their children, and teach the parents some of the coping skills that their children are learning.

These intervention models have proven able to prevent

or reduce the post-divorce behavior problems which some children experience at home and at school. Pedro-Carroll's program specifically evaluated whether her support group program would reduce children's problems in school. Teachers of group participants reported that after completing the support group their students showed far fewer shy-anxious behaviors and learning problems, and significantly improved in other social skills such as peer sociability, frustration tolerance, compliance with rules, and adaptive assertiveness (Pedro-Carroll & Cowan, 1985).

These program evaluations share two major limitations. First, the evaluations did not compare the academic performance of the children before and after they participated in the group. As a consequence, no one has actually proved that support groups improve participants' grades or achievement test scores, though the groups do improve participants' behavior in school. Second, these program models have only been tested on predominantly white, middle-class, suburban children. To remedy this second problem, the Rochester, New York program is currently being refined and adapted for use in urban schools for children from varied socioeconomic backgrounds, and for children going through other kinds of family crises.

Other School Programs for One-Parent Children. Well-designed and well-run divorce groups are helpful in reducing divorce-related stress in children, but they do not claim to meet all of the school needs of one-parent children. Children experiencing a parent's divorce may need additional homework assistance, as well as a support group experience. On the other hand, some one-parent children who are not experiencing a family crisis still need some extra time and attention from adults at school. One-parent children need help specific to their particular situation rather than some generic assistance provided for all one-parent students.

A Comprehensive Approach. Some schools are presently offering more comprehensive programs for children from one-parent families. One such program is based in the Hamden, Connecticut school district. In Hamden, a school social worker, Jane Strauss, and a community mental health specialist, John McGann, have developed a program based on an "ecological" perspective. Their view is that when a family in crisis is unable to meet a child's needs, other institutions in the child's community network of social supports, such as the child's school, should step in to help the child.

The Hamden program is designed to create a school-based community support system for children (Linney & Vemberg, 1983). First, workshops are held for teachers and other school staff on how to provide in-school support to one-parent children. Second, workshops at PTA meetings instruct the wider parent community about one-parent families and create community support for additional services (i.e., after-school child care) and greater sensitivity towards one-parent children (i.e., changing father/child events into parent/child events). Third, a structured children's support group helps one-parent children in crisis cope with their problems, and an evening single parents' support group meets to discuss single-parenting issues. Finally, special classroom programs teach children about different family types and about family changes like separation and divorce.

Hamden's comprehensive school program incorporates assistance for single parents as well as for their children. This is a valid approach to the school problems of one-parent children. A single parent's ability to provide a positive home environment and to become actively involved in his or her child's school work greatly influences the child's school performance. The next chapter will discuss in more detail the ways in which schools can support these single parents' efforts to help their children achieve in school.

Chapter Five:

SCHOOL RELATIONS WITH SINGLE PARENTS

In the last chapter we learned that children from all family types can do well in school if they have parental support at home. This support includes providing for basic needs such as food, shelter, and clothing as well as basic care of the child's health and emotional well-being. But parents can be directly involved in their children's education in several other ways as well: by meeting with their child's teacher to review their child's progress, by helping their child with homework, by attending school activities, by volunteering to help on school outings or projects, and by getting involved in school policy issues through parent/teacher organizations and parent advisory councils (Epstein, 1986).

It is important to remember that like other parents, single parents vary in their interests and ability to participate in their children's education. They have different levels of education, financial resources, occupational status, and self-esteem, all of which influence their efforts to help their children academically (Epstein, 1986). Some single parents are indistinguishable from two-parent couples in the extent to which they are involved in their children's education, even though it is harder for them to find the time. A common complaint from these single parents is that they don't receive enough credit from school officials for their contributions to their children's education. This project found that single parents don't always command the same respect that couples receive from school administrators.

We are also concerned with those single parents who lack the resources to help their children in school. They may lack the income to provide the basics for their children. They may work full-time and lack the time to attend school activities. They may be experiencing an emotional crisis and therefore lack the ability to meet their children's emotional needs. As the past chapters have indicated, many single parents are under great personal stress as they attempt to raise their children alone with limited resources under trying conditions. This chapter will examine the ways in which schools can help these single parents support their children's education. We do not mean to imply that schools should take over parents' roles when parents don't get involved in school. But we offer some ways in which schools can bolster single parents' efforts to help their children achieve in school.

Child-Centered Assistance

Basic Finances. Not all single parents can provide their children with the basic shelter, clothing, nutrition, and medical care that children need to perform well in school. Although parents in both one-parent and two-parent families can lack the financial resources to provide adequately for their children, one-parent families are much poorer, averaging one-third the annual income of two-parent families. Single parents are therefore often less able to meet their children's basic needs. Schools can help these low-income families by offering free or subsidized school breakfast and lunch programs, and by being sensitive to families who seem to be in financial trouble, referring them promptly to the appropriate family assistance agency.

Many single parents who work full-time and are not at home to prepare breakfast or lunch for their children also depend on school meal programs to ensure that their children eat properly. One mother we interviewed pointed out that the availability of school meals is necessary but not always sufficient. As we all know, children cannot be forced to eat unappetizing food. And children who are under severe stress may not be eating anything at all. This mother suggested that school staff let parents know when their child was not eating. In schools where many children are refusing to eat school meals, it may be necessary to re-examine the entire food preparation program.

Child Care. Many working single parents share with two-parent families the problem of finding care for their children during non-school hours. This includes routine occasions: before and after school, on school holidays and in-service days, and during summer vacations; and unexpected occasions: when children are sick, when children are suspended from school, or when bad weather forces schools to close.

Child care has special relevance for single parents who lack the resources of two-parent families. Two working parents have twice as much vacation leave available to take care of their children's emergencies, and can more easily afford to pay for child care. And as we mentioned in the first chapter, single parents more often work full-time (41 percent) than do both parents in a two-parent family (27 percent). For these reasons child care issues are especially critical for single parents.

Working single parents often have a hard time finding adequate before-school and after-school child care. Arranging for child care on unexpected occasions is even more difficult, and single parents cannot always miss work themselves. According to the director of a Brooklyn child care center, emergency child care for sick children is the biggest problem facing the single parents in his low-income Hispanic neighborhood. These parents fear they will be fired from their factory jobs if they miss another day of work, and yet they have nowhere to place their sick children.

In our focus group interviews we heard about school-related child care problems from many of the mothers. A never-married mother described her son's daily trip to an early-morning sitter which tired him out before the beginning of the school day. A divorced mother complained that the school staff's preferred method for handling her young son's behavior problems was to call her at work and ask her to take him home, even though she could not afford to leave work for the day. A widow with four school-age children told us that she eventually had to quit her job when it came to the point of being absent from work several times in a week to take care of her children. A never-married woman in one focus group described the system of phone calls that she uses as a stop-gap measure to keep track of her son who stays home alone after school.

Latchkey Children. All the full-time working mothers in our focus groups worried about finding acceptable child care for their children and having to leave their children alone at times. Evidence suggests that many of the children who end up caring for themselves as "latchkey" children come from one-parent families. In one study of 60 white, middle-class families with children between the ages of six and twelve, more than half of the children of divorced, working mothers stayed home alone after school an average of an hour and a half each day. In contrast, less than half of the two-parent children in the study stayed home alone after school (Devall, Soneman, & Brody, 1986). It is estimated that by 1990 there may be as many as six million "latchkey" children who are on their own after school, on weekends, and during holidays while their parents work (Robinson, Rowland, & Coleman, 1986).

Controversy exists over whether or not latchkey status is a problem for children. While some older elementary school-age children do not need child care, researchers find that others cannot handle the latchkey situation. In general, experts advise parents not to leave children home alone under the age of ten (Conroy, 1988). Parents are apprehensive about latchkey arrangements, and worry that their children will get into trouble when left at home alone.

How children fare in a latchkey situation seems to depend as much on the safety of their environment as on their own maturity. Studies of children in inner-city black neighborhoods have reported that more than 30 percent of the children in self-care had high fear levels, while studies of white middle-class children in rural or suburban settings found much lower fear levels (Robinson, Rowland, & Coleman, 1986). We interviewed children from the poor Brooklyn neighborhood of Flatbush who did not want their classmates to know about their single-parent status because they worried about being followed home after school.

Child Care Shortage Concerns Teachers. Recently the lack of child care for school-age children has become a major concern among teachers. A 1987 nation-wide Harris poll of 1,000 public school teachers and 2,000 parents of public school students found that the teachers singled out children's being left alone at home after school as the major cause of students' having difficulty in school (Harris, 1987). In fact, more teachers saw this as the critical factor in students' school troubles than saw poverty and single-parent families as key, although the issues of poverty, single-parent families, and latchkey care are related. In this poll, 41 percent of the parents reported that their children are sometimes on their own between the end of school and 5:30 P.M. Fifty-nine percent of the parents agreed with the teachers' criticism that "most" parents leave their children too much on their own after school (Harris, 1987).

Child Care Solutions. A majority of parents, especially single parents, advocate school-based child care as an appropriate solution. In the 1981 National Committee for Citizens in Education survey of single parents, 64 percent of the parents felt that schools should provide child care before and after school hours (Conway & Mechler, 1983). More recently, the 1987 Harris survey of teachers and parents found that a majority of the parents polled expressed a willingness to use an after-school program organized for students by the school. This interest in after-school programs was not confined to parents who worked or who had latchkey children. A majority (52 percent) of all the parents polled indicated that they would be willing to pay extra for such programs if necessary (Harris, 1987).

Communities, schools in particular, have responded slowly to parental interest in school-based child care. Educators argue that schools cannot assume complete responsibility for latchkey children. Instead, they have encouraged parent and community groups to develop their own services for school-age children. Child care researchers Linney & Vemberg report, "Although some schools have extended-day programs, it is up to parents to locate, barter for, or purchase the necessary services outside of school" (Linney & Vemberg, 1983).

A variety of community programs have been created as a result. For example, in the Midwest there are now neighborhood "safe homes" programs where children who need emergency help can go to houses on their block that display "helping hand" signs in the window. In the California Safety Pals program, high school students give "latchkey survival training" presentations to grade school students. Similar "survival" lessons which teach children how to call 911 in emergencies, how to cook simple meals, and how to handle simple medical problems, have been created for use in classrooms and even for use in early-morning television shows for kids. Some communities have started homework assistance hot lines, latchkey help hot lines, and community-based after-school programs (Robinson, Rowland, & Coleman, 1986).

Increasingly, community groups are using (leasing, borrowing) school facilities to provide school-age child care (Henderson, et al., 1986). In New York City, for example, the YMCA and YWCA have organized after-school and summer camp programs in public elementary schools throughout the city's five boroughs. We interviewed single-parent children in three of these summer camps and learned that parents must pay or obtain scholarships for their children to attend such community programs. This can certainly be a hardship for some single parents.

Parent-Centered Assistance

Parenting Support. When single parents feel overwhelmed by their responsibilities, they often need extra help in order to help their children in school. All of the teachers we interviewed concurred with a colleague's comment that "something must be done for the parent. You can do everything possible for the kids in school, but the key is the parent." These teachers argued that schools should help parents who need support in raising their children and in contributing to a positive school experience. Rather than counseling parents directly, they suggested that schools help parents by developing a list of community mental health and single-parenting resources which teachers and guidance counselors can use to refer parents to appropriate support services.

Several of the single mothers we interviewed who relied on social service agencies for assistance argued that schools ought to serve as sources of community program information. Many stressed single parents are isolated socially and unaware of available family support services. Their children's school may be one of their few links to the local community and one of their few sources of information. As evidence of the problems single parents have obtaining such information, the mothers in each of the focus groups eagerly exchanged telephone numbers of their favorite community programs.

Community Support Programs. Many communities are fortunate enough to have a large number and variety of programs that can give single parents who may be feeling isolated and overwhelmed the social supports and practical guidance needed to help them handle their parenting responsibilities. These programs include parenting support groups in mental health centers, parenting classes, single-parent networks, and church or synagogue programs for recently widowed or divorced people (Drake, 1981). One of the largest and best known self-help organizations for single parents is Parents Without Partners, a national organization with over a thousand chapters and 150,000 members (Benedek & Benedek, 1979). It offers single parents practical help through its *Single Parent* magazine and companionship through social events and informal discussion groups.

Researchers Burns & Brassard argue that the social isolation which is common among single parents can damage their emotional health and their relationships with their children, especially when children are trying to adapt to life in a one-parent family (Burns & Brassard, 1982). Divorce is an especially isolating experience for parents and for children, but this sense of isolation can be lessened by making connections with other single-parents families and building a network of support (Rich, 1988). Tina Birnbaum, the director of Parenthesis, a Chicago support group for single mothers, praised the supportive role of these groups, saying that "the most important thing you can do for high-risk single-parent families is to provide support for the parents. . . When the mothers feel supported, not isolated, they do a better job of parenting."

School Counseling for Parents. Direct school intervention may be needed in communities where there are few outside supports for single parents and in situations where parents request assistance from school staff. Some experts argue that if parents are so distraught that they are unable to cope, they should be able to discuss their problems with friends, relatives, child care staff, or teachers, and they should be assured that it is acceptable to ask school personnel for help. Teachers are in a key position to know when this help is needed. In talking with parents, teachers can help by acknowledging the parents' pain, but must avoid stigmatizing them (Appel).

School Support Groups. Several education experts have recommended that school social workers or psychologists do more for single parents than listen sympathetically to their problems. Trained school professionals should run evening single-parent support groups at school to enable single parents to share their experiences and receive emotional support from each other, and also learn some practical parenting skills (Burns & Brassard, 1982).

There are many kinds of single-parent groups now in the schools, with the content and format of each group depending somewhat on the group's goals. Some groups are lecture series, where experts discuss subjects of importance to single parents such as the legal issues surrounding divorce, child custody, and the rights of non-custodial parents to school records. In other groups, educators teach single parents problem-solving techniques, stress management, management of financial resources, and job search skills (Worell, 1986). In a third kind of support group, leaders encourage parents to share their personal experiences and to help each other on practical problems.

For example, a school-based group for divorced parents called the HELPING model was developed in the early 1980's as a "multimodal" intervention for parents and children. It addresses health, emotional well-being, single-parent family lifestyles, personal relationships, self-image, and problem-solving issues. This eight-session program has parents and children meeting in separate rooms and learning through discussions, skills-training sessions, and media presentations (Green, 1981).

Schools can also help single parents create their own school-based single-parent support networks. One mother we interviewed suggested that single parents meet to set up baby-sitting cooperatives and arrange late afternoon transportation for their children, who otherwise might not be able to participate in after-school activities. They can also organize themselves to create a stronger voice for single-parent interests in school affairs.

Through their children's schools, single parents can also join together to set up social activities for themselves and/or their children. Dorothy Rich, of the Home and School Institute, suggests many kinds of inexpensive and enjoyable school-based social supports for single parents. They include movie nights, potlucks, family talent shows, cultural outings, clothing exchanges, and parent/child school activities on Saturdays when non-custodial parents also have a chance to be involved (Rich, 1988).

This section has outlined several ways in which schools can help, or find help for, single parents who are having trouble providing for their families' basic needs. In the rest of the chapter we will examine how well schools are involving one-parent families in school activities.

Single Parents' Involvement in School

Education expert Joyce Epstein argues that there are four ways in which schools and parents work together to enhance the education of their children. First, schools and parents are obliged to communicate regarding the children's school performance. Beyond this basic level, parents can become involved in school in three different ways—volunteering for school projects, assisting their children's learning activities at home, and serving in parent/teacher organizations and parent advisory councils (Epstein, 1986).

School/Home Communication. School staff use a variety of means to communicate with parents, including report cards, parent/teacher conferences, notices, and school news-letters (Clay, 1981). School officials also meet with parents at school activities such as student performances and events, and school board meetings. Traditionally, personal contacts between parents and school officials occurred during school hours on the assumption that mothers, as homemakers, were available to meet during the day. Meetings during school hours are very inconvenient for working parents, many of whom are single parents. In the 1981 National Committee for Citizens in Education survey of single parents, 45 percent of those surveyed said they had to leave work in order to attend parent/teacher conferences (Clay, 1981).

There are some indications that in the last ten years schools have begun to adjust to working parents' schedules. In her 1985 study concerning parent involvement in schools, Anne Henderson reported that most schools now have ways to communicate with families that have no parent at home during the day. The new methods include more flexible meet-ing times (evening and weekend hours) and greater use of the telephone for parent/teacher conferences (Henderson, et al., 1986). But there is little more than anecdotal information currently available about how many schools have adapted their schedules to the time constraints of working and single parents (Clay, 1981).

The evidence we found suggested that while some schools have successfully adapted their school activity sched-ules for working parents, others have made little or no effort to do so. For example, the 1987 Harris poll of American teachers and parents found a significant mismatch in their preferred meeting schedules. While nine out of ten teachers surveyed reported that traditional afternoon meeting times were most convenient to them, only 9 percent preferred to see parents in the evening. On the other hand, one-third (36 percent) of the parents employed full-time preferred to meet teachers in the evening. This created a work conflict for most of the full-time working parents (44 percent of all the parents polled). Seventy-one percent of the single parents employed full-time and 62 percent of the single parents employed part-time said that they had taken time off work to visit their children's school.

Several of the single mothers we interviewed said that their schools continue to schedule parent-related activities during the school day. One single working mother talked about having to leave her job one weekday morning in order to pick up candy for the school candy drive. The only pickup time was between 9:00 A.M. and 11:00 A.M. on a school day. Another single mother mentioned that her school made an effort to accommodate working parents by scheduling one evening each term for parent/teacher conferences, but no other evening appointments were available for parents who had conflicts that evening. Parents with time conflicts were required to make day-time appointments.

On the other hand, we learned of individual teachers and guidance counselors who conscientiously rearranged their schedules and made themselves available to working parents in other ways. One of the focus group elementary school teachers (who was also a single parent) mentioned that she provides her home telephone number to parents at the beginning of the school year. She denied being overwhelmed by parent calls and felt that this was a good way for teachers to help parents. According to Susan Diamond, the guidance counselors in her Scarsdale, New York public high school also worked out an early morning schedule so that working parents can visit a counselor between 7:30 and 9:00 A.M. These arrangements are important steps for schools to take to help working parents, especially single working parents, stay informed and involved in their child's education.

Non-Custodial Parent/School Relations. In the past schools have seldom taken the lead in communicating with non-custodial parents. Under the U.S. Family Educational Rights and Privacy Act of 1974 (FERPA), non-custodial parents have legal access to their child's school records unless there is a legally binding agreement which specifically removes the non-custodial parent's right to know about the child's educational progress. However, we learned from single-parent organization representatives that many schools do not routinely offer these parents the opportunity to view their child's school records. Indeed, some schools refuse to let them see the records. Our project uncovered no studies documenting the extent to which schools are complying with the law. The 1981 National Committee for Citizens in Education survey reported, though, that less than 7 percent of the non-custodial parents received their child's report cards (Clay, 1981).

Sometimes schools get caught in custody battles between divorcing parents and are reluctant to go against the custodial parent's wishes. In one focus group, a separated mother in the midst of a custody battle said that she, the custodial parent, threatened to sue the school if it released any school records to the father. In these cases the federal law clearly protects the right of non-custodial parents to have access to their child's academic records. Schools that refuse parents' access without the authority to do so violate the law. Other forms of school information that are not addressed by FERPA regulations include fliers about school activities, emergency telephone calls, and school year calendars, all of which help to keep non-custodial parents informed and interested in their child's education. Schools have been even more reluctant to pass along this additional information than to send report cards to non-custodial parents.

Staying informed about school events and activities is one of the few ways non-custodial parents can continue to participate in their children's education. Research has revealed the importance of this information, finding that having both parents interested and involved in school helps to give a child the confidence and motivation to do well. But schools have rarely recognized the positive role that non-custodial parents can play in their child's education. Divorced-parent groups charge that exclusion of non-custodial parents from school activities is widespread, and is one of the most common complaints that bring people into fathers' rights groups (Brooks, 1984). In the past, some non-custodial parents have had to take their child's school to court in order to obtain information about their child's school activities.

Some schools make a point of informing divorced and separated families about their legal rights to school records, and actively involve non-custodial parents in parent/teacher conferences and other important school events. For example, the Scarsdale, New York school district publishes its non-custodial parent school records policy in the first parent newsletter of the school year. Also, one of the elementary school teachers we interviewed described holding separate conferences for both parents in divorced families. We encourage schools to do more of this type of activity.

Parents as Tutors. There has been a major movement to bring parents into the education process in creative and innovative ways, demonstrating the efforts of many schools to enhance student achievement (Linney & Vemberg, 1983). Although few studies have looked at the specific levels and forms of parent involvement which help children most, parental involvement appears to be beneficial to children's performance and adjustment to school. For pre-school and elementary school children, parental involvement most enhances school achievement when parents directly tutor their children and monitor their homework. In the elementary and middle school grades and beyond, an effective parent role is that of supplementing the child's school work with cultural and recreational experiences.

Although parent involvement is one of the most often cited elements of effective schools, it is one of the least understood (Epstein, 1986). Teacher training typically does not address parent involvement practices, and so teachers have little help with ways to involve parents. To encourage parents to help their children with school work at home, researcher Joyce Epstein has developed a TIPS program designed to give elementary school teachers a process for involving all parents in their children's homework activities.

Parent/Teacher Conflicts. Researchers report that single parents find it difficult to participate in their children's education, while schools have not been sensitive to their time and resource constraints (Stedman, 1987). Part of the problem seems to be that teachers have expectations for single parents that the parents find hard to meet. For example, some single parents have trouble setting aside time on short notice to assist with homework that is assigned one day and due the next. Some single parents may also not have the time every day to check over their children's work. In separated or divorced families where the children spend their weekends at their non-custodial parent's house, homework assignments can get lost in the shuffle. Working single parents may also not be able to take time off work to attend day-time teacher conferences. Single parents recognize that they do not always have the time and energy to do everything teachers expect of them (Epstein, 1984).

These scheduling problems and mismatches between teacher expectations and single-parent involvement can cause conflict between teachers and parents and contribute to teachers' negative attitudes about single parents. Teachers who do not understand single-parent family situations often become concerned about single parents' apparent neglect of their child's education, especially when they see undone homework assignments and non-attendance at parent/ teacher conferences (Burns & Brassard, 1982).

Joyce Epstein's 1984 survey of 1,269 parents, 24 percent of whom were single parents, analyzed the differences between elementary school relations with one-parent and two-parent families. The study found that although both married and single parents were concerned about their children's education and worked with their children on homework activities, married parents spent significantly more time than single parents in school as volunteers and classroom helpers and at PTA meetings. Married parents had more familiarity with school personnel in part because their children attended the same school longer than one-parent children. Married parents also had more resources than single parents for home-learning activities—more books, more personal reading time, and higher education levels. Significantly and surprisingly, although single parents had less time available for their children, especially if they had more than one child, and to assist at school, they felt more pressure than married parents to assist their children at home and they spent more time on home educational activities than married parents (Epstein, 1984).

Epstein's study found that teachers who were considered "leaders" in the frequent use of organized parent-involvement activities (reading assistance, informal learning games, drills of basic skills, and tutoring activities, etc.) had higher opinions of single parents than teachers who were not considered to be such leaders. Teachers who were non-leaders rated single parents significantly lower than married parents in helpfulness and in follow-through on home-learning activities, even after parents' education levels, levels of parent involvement at school, the child's classroom achievement, and other important variables were taken into account (Epstein, 1984). Non-leaders also held significantly lower opinions of the quality of the homework of one-parent children than two-parent children, regardless of the child's academic achievement level.

There are several potential explanations for the differences between leader and non-leader attitudes towards single-parent families. Teachers who work actively with parents may get to know single parents and their special circumstances well enough to change their pre-conceptions about these parents, or they may find new ways to help these parents get more involved in their children's education. Single parents who get involved in home-learning activities may also have an easier time meeting the teacher's expectations. Sometimes all that single parents need is some understanding of their time constraints. For example, the mothers in our focus groups requested more than one day's notice of homework assignments from their children's teachers. A weekly homework schedule, they said, would enable them to plan their time to allow for help with homework when needed.

Parent Advocacy. Another aspect of parental involvement is parent participation in school policy issues, again an area where single parents have time and resource constraints. In some school districts, the school board meets at an inconvenient time. Even when meetings are scheduled in the evenings, child care is rarely provided.

Some single parents do not have any extra time or energy to follow school politics, and so are at a disadvantage should they wish to speak out on certain topics. One focus group mother explained that she had been active in her school's parent/teacher organization until her divorce, when she temporarily dropped out of all outside activities. She later had trouble getting accepted back into her school's group of active parents because of her earlier absence.

The focus group mothers suggested several feasible ways to increase single-parent involvement in school policy matters. Besides making school board and parent/teacher organization meeting times more convenient and providing child care during meetings, schools should make meeting minutes available for parents unable to come to the meetings. These mothers also requested more respect from school administrators when they do speak up on policy issues concerning their children, feeling that married couples and single fathers receive more attention.

Volunteers. Many single parents want to support their child's school but cannot afford more than a token effort on school projects. Several of the mothers we interviewed said that they would be able to do more if their schools let them know in advance about important events so that they could save the time off work.

This chapter has sketched some important ways in which single parents and schools can better work together to improve the education of their children. In the next chapter, our final recommendations for elementary schools will attempt to combine the ideas proposed thus far into a comprehensive program for one-parent families.

Chapter Six:

CONCLUSION AND RECOMMENDATIONS

American public schools are caught in a dilemma. Schools have limited resources with which to serve a student population that has changed dramatically over the last few decades to include a much higher proportion of students considered to be "high risks" for academic failure: children from low-income families, non-white families, and one-parent families. This report has investigated the educational needs of one group—elementary school-age children from one-parent families—and found that these children and their families have somewhat different needs than the two-parent children who have traditionally populated American schools.

We found that one-parent children and their families varied greatly in their background characteristics and educational needs. One-parent children who live in wealthy, well-educated, emotionally stable family situations tend not to have the school problems of children from financially struggling families or from families in the midst of an emotional crisis. It is important for schools to recognize, however, that one-parent families are much more likely to be under emotional and economic stress than two-parent families. In this final chapter we will discuss how schools, given their resource constraints, can best serve one-parent students.

Certain family and school conditions create a learning environment that helps children, regardless of their family status, perform to their full potential. Children who do well in school come from families in which parents clearly value school, give children guidance and encouragement with their schoolwork, and provide an organized and predictable home life. Children also excel in schools where there is a safe, orderly, disciplined environment, regular and frequent reviews of a child's progress, and teachers who maintain high expectations that all students can and will learn.

The central problem is that these optimal school and home conditions do not exist for many one-parent children. Many single parents are under considerable financial and emotional stress as they attempt to cope with full-time work and solo parenting responsibilities; some parents have family trauma to cope with as well. These parents often have trouble providing their children with the educational support they need in the form of a stable home environment, adequate child care, schoolwork assistance, and regular contact with their children's teachers. On the other hand, many schools fail one-parent students by not adapting to their families' needs. Many schools maintain inconvenient meeting and conference schedules and many school personnel continue to hold negative images and low expectations for students and parents from one-parent families. In these schools, many single-parent children fall behind academically and never catch up.

Recommendations

We propose that schools offer five kinds of assistance to one-parent families. Each category includes a complex of concrete policies and programs, many of which are mentioned throughout the report but are also listed in Appendix Two. We recommend the following:

1. Sensitivity and respect of one-parent family circumstances and needs.
2. An "early warning" system to identify and assist children in academic trouble.
3. One-parent family support programs.
4. Affordable school-based child care.
5. Classroom practices and parent involvement activities that support one-parent children's learning efforts.

1. **Sensitivity**: The first step is for school personnel to accept the presence and special needs of one-parent families. We believe that schools must change from viewing one-parent families as abnormal and problematic to viewing these families as worthy of the same respect and consideration that two-parent families enjoy. We found many schools in which the school administrators and staff had successfully increased their sensitivity towards one-parent family issues. The methods these schools used to learn about the needs of their districts' one-parent families varied: Here are some examples:

One focus group teacher told us that her school revamped its single-parent family policies after a guest speaker conducted an in-service workshop concerning one-parent families. In two other examples, in Pennsylvania and New Jersey, the school district's head school psychologist became interested in the subject when he noticed an increase in the number of troubled one-parent families. In one case, the psychologist conducted a formal needs-assessment survey of the district's single parents. In the other case, the person held a PTA meeting for single parents and recorded the parents' concerns. Both then initiated children's and parents' support groups in elementary schools.

In a wealthy, private Manhattan school, a group of divorced parents lobbied the school to provide more services for one-parent children. Another focus group teacher told us how she requested and received permission to lead informal "rap sessions" on family issues at her public school for the children (mostly from one-parent families) who stayed after school in an extra-curricular activity program.

2. **An "Early Warning" System.** The second step for schools is to be alert to children's family status and circumstances and to assist one-parent families as soon as trouble occurs. When school personnel are aware of family-status changes they can offer more appropriate assistance to troubled students.

We have found school administrators who have organized efficient information tracking systems that record status changes for both custodial and non-custodial parents. School secretaries who take parent calls and messages often know about family changes before other school personnel and can be tapped for updating family information on student records. A simple family status change card can also accompany each student's report card. Several single-parent school guides have published sample student record forms that include questions about custodial and non-custodial parents' names, addresses, and telephone numbers.

This monitoring of one-parent students should lead to scheduling parent/teacher conferences at convenient times, talking with parents about problems that crop up (unfinished homework, sudden behavior changes, etc.), and referring parents to school psychologists or community assistance agencies, when appropriate. One focus group teacher said she gave her home telephone number to all her students' parents so that they can reach her in an emergency. In the Montour, Pennsylvania school district, counselors are assigned to track certain students who are having problems by checking daily that each student is in school and has completed his or her homework.

3. One-Parent Family Support Programs. The third step is for schools to offer school-based programs or to work with community agencies that assist one-parent families in crisis. Some parents and children greatly benefit from school-based support groups. Other parents and children need more intensive help than a school has the time, staff, or expertise to provide. Schools have found ways, however, to help families receive the social services—counseling, after-school child care, health care, etc.—that they need.

In the New York City area, several school districts have trained elementary school teachers and counselors to lead children's support groups at school. In other New York and Pennsylvania school systems, school staff gave initial planning support to help parents form their own single-parent interest groups. In a Virginia district, the school administrators allowed a researcher to start up and test a combined parent/child support group model on the condition that the researcher leave behind a self-sustaining program. One focus group teacher from the Bronx described a Big Brothers and Big Sisters program (which matches one-parent children with teen-age or adult parent substitutes) that is administered in the school.

4. Affordable School-Based Child Care. In addition to offering child care during school-sponsored activities, schools should work with community agencies to provide before- and after-school child care for low-income children from one-parent homes. If a school lacks enough resources to run a school-based child care program, administrators can still help by volunteering school space, organizing high school student volunteers, and permitting the use of school equipment for before-school and after-school child care activities. In New York City, for example, some public elementary schools have opened their doors to independent community-based after-school programs.

5. Classroom Practices. A final step for schools to take in a comprehensive program for one-parent children is to encourage the use of lessons, classroom activities, and children's stories that reflect the school's demographics. Children feel better about themselves and their families when they do not feel different from their classmates. Active parent involvement programs also help single-parent families feel more welcome at school and engaged in the education process.

We do not necessarily recommend that schools immediately purchase a whole new set of textbooks, although schools should pressure publishers to update their readers to include non-traditional families. Creative alternatives to textbooks are school library collections about one-parent families and story-telling opportunities where children describe their own families. One focus group fourth-grader commented that the only story she had read about one-parent families was written by a classmate for a story writing contest. School teachers and librarians can readily obtain children's book bibliographies from organizations, such as Parents Without Partners, which are listed in Appendix One.

Appendix One:

RESOURCES: EXPERTS AND ORGANIZATIONS

Banana Splits Program
Liz McGonagle, Counselor
Woods Road Elementary School
Ballston Spa, NY 12020
(518) 885–5361

Andrea H. Beller
Division of Family and Consumer Economics
University of Illinois (Urbana-Champaign)
274 Bevier Hall
905 South Goodwin Ave.
Urbana, IL 61801–3898
(217) 333–1000

Gwenyth Britton
School of Education
Education Hall—Room 308
Oregon State University
Corvallis, OR 97330
(503) 754–0123

Florence Cherry
Family Development Center
Dept. of Human Ecology
Cornell University
Ithaca, NY 14851
(607) 255–2537

CCAC
Child Care Action Campaign
Donna Euben
99 Hudson St.
Room 1233
New York, NY 10013
(212) 334–9595

Child Trends
Christine Moore
2100 M St. NW
Suite 411
Washington, DC 20037
(202) 223–6288

Children's Defense Fund
122 C St. NW
Washington, DC 20001
(202) 483–1470

Paul Ciborowski
Support Group Facilitator
Sachem High School
212 Smith Road
Lake Ronkonkoma, NY 11779
(516) 467–0417

Congressional Research Service
James Stedman, Specialist in Education
Education and Public Welfare Division
The Library of Congress
Washington, DC 20540
(202) 707–5700

Susan A. Diamond
Scarsdale High School
Brewster Road
Scarsdale, NY 10583
(914) 723–5500

Divorce Equity, Inc.
3130 Mayfield Rd.
Cleveland Heights, OH 44118
(216) 321–8587

Joyce Epstein
Center for Research on Elementary and Middle Schools
Johns Hopkins University
3505 N. Charles St.
Baltimore, MD 21218
(301) 338–7570

Family Education Center Library
Helen Beckwith, Librarian
Greater Plains Elementary School
Oneonta, NY 13820
(607) 433–8272

Family Resource Coalition
230 North Michigan Ave.
Suite 1625
Chicago, IL 60601
(312) 726–4750

Family Rights and Privacy Act
U.S. Dept. of Education
Room 4512 Switzer Bldg.
Washington, DC 20005
(202) 245–0233

Martha Frost, Ed.D.
The Schools and Single-Parent Families Project
Center for Human Resources
State University of NY
Plattsburgh, NY 12901
(518) 564–4173

Mary Lou Fuller
Center for Teaching and Learning
University of North Dakota
Grand Forks, ND 58202
(701) 777–2674

Harvard Family Research Project
Kathryn Parsons
Gutman Library 301
Appian Way
Cambridge, MA 02138
(617) 495–9108

E. Mavis Hetherington
Dept. of Psychology
University of Virginia
Charlottesville, VA 22903
(804) 924–3374

Home and School Institute
Dorothy Rich, President
Special Projects Office
1201 16th St. NW
Washington, DC 20036
(202) 466–3633

Kindred Spirits
250 W. 57th St.
Suite 1527
New York, NY 10019
(212) 427–6000

NAESP
National Association of Elementary Principals
1801 N. Moore St.
Arlington, VA 22209
(703) 684–3345

NCCE
National Committee for Citizens in Education
Nancy Burla
410 Wilde Lake Village Green
Columbia, MD 21044
(800) 638–9675

NCFR
The National Council on Family Relations
1910 West County Road B
Roseville, MN 55113
(612) 633–6933

The National Parent Teacher Association
Manya Ungar, President
700 North Rush St.
Chicago, IL 60611
(312) 787–0977

Parenthesis Parent-Child Center
Nancy Waichler, Executive Director
405 South Euclid Avenue
Oak Park, IL 60302
(312) 848–2227

Parents Without Partners, Inc.
Ginna Muta, President
7910 Woodmont Ave.
Suite 1000
Bethesda, MD 20814
(301) 654–8850

Joann Pedro-Carroll
University of Rochester
575 Mount Hope Ave.
Rochester, NY 14620
(716) 275–2547

School-Age Child Care Project
Michelle Seligson, Director
Wellesley College Center for Research on Women
828 Washington St.
Wellesley, MA 02181
(617) 235–0320

Single Mothers By Choice
200 East 84th Street
New York, NY 10028
(212) 988–0993

Single Parents Resource Center
Suzanne Jones, Exec. Director
1165 Broadway—Room 504
New York, NY 10001
(212) 213–0047

Sisterhood of Black Single Mothers
Barbara Christian, Director
1360 Fulton Street
Brooklyn, NY 11216
(718) 638–0413

The Step-Family Association of America, Inc.
28 Allegheny Ave.
Suite 1307
Baltimore, MD 21204
(301) 823–7570

Arnold Stolberg
Dept. of Psychology
Virginia Commonwealth University
806 W. Franklin St.
Richmond, VA 23284–2018
(804) 367–1179

Bernard Sulkowski
Assistant Superintendent
Montour School District
5501 Steubenville Pike
McKees Rocks, PA 15136
(412) 787–1060

Judith Wallerstein
Center for the Family in Transition
5725 Paradise Drive
Corte Madera, CA 94925
(415) 924–5750

Appendix Two:

SPECIFIC SUGGESTIONS

The policy recommendations listed below come from parents, teachers, and school administrators who have worked extensively with single-parent families. Some of the suggestions have already been published in several excellent school guides, including: *Single Parents and Their Families: A Guide to Involving School and Community,* by the National PTA in conjunction with Boys Town and the National Association of Elementary School Principals; *Schools, Single Parents and Their Children,* an information sheet by Parents Without Partners, Inc.; and *Helping Children of Divorce,* written by Susan Arnsberg Diamond. Other ideas came from the education experts and focus group participants interviewed during this project. The suggestions are categorized below according to the five main recommendation sections outlined in Chapter Six.

Sensitivity Towards One-Parent Families

1. Offer an in-service workshop to school teachers, staff, and administrators which:

- provides information about changing family population patterns,
- allows school personnel to examine their own attitudes, values, and stereotypes,
- alerts them to direct and indirect forms of discrimination against one-parent families, and

- teaches them how to provide support to and to recognize signs of distress in children in crisis.

2. Review school policies and practices regarding one-parent families. The review may consider some of the following questions:

- Does the school hold events such as father-son dinners that might make one-parent children uncomfortable?
- Are school notices sent to "mother and father" rather than to "dear parent or guardian?"
- Do non-custodial parents have access to their child's records as allowed by federal law (FERPA)?
- Do school personnel describe one-parent families as "broken homes" or use other derogatory terms?
- Are school activities scheduled at times inconvenient to working parents?
- Do school texts reflect current family life?

3. Ask parents and teachers what community services exist and additional school services are needed for one-parent families.

- Is there enough affordable school-age child care available or are there long waiting lists?
- What family support and counseling services do local churches, synagogues, and community agencies provide?
- Do local community education centers offer parenting education courses that address single-parent concerns?
- What do one-parent families need from school?

4. Organize a PTA meeting regarding single-parent issues that introduces the topic of one-parent families to the entire school community. Make this an opportunity for single parents to meet each other and work together on other events for one-parent families.

An Early Warning System

1. Review the school's record-keeping system to see whether information about children's family status is complete and up-to-date. School records should include the following:

- Full names, addresses, marital status, and home and work telephone numbers of the child's custodial and non-custodial parents,
- Full names, addresses, and telephone numbers of other adults in the child's household, including step-parents, significant others, and grandparents,
- Instructions in case of illness, injury, or emergency school closing,
- List of persons authorized to pick the child up at school,
- Name of person financially responsible for the child,
- Indication of whether duplicate notices and report cards are necessary.

2. The teacher should get to know the child's family early in the school year, before any problems occur, through a first week parent/teacher conference or parent night. One way to establish and maintain contact with busy working parents is for the teacher to offer a home telephone number for emergencies.

3. Frequently review the child's progress with both parents through telephone or in-person conferences. Inform the parents of any classroom behavior problems or signs of distress in the child's school activities, try to learn the reason for any behavior changes, and offer referrals to other school or outside professionals, if required for the child.

4. Maintain a list of community programs for one-parent families. Distribute the information to all school staff, set up a community bulletin board about special events and meetings, and inform parents through a school newsletter or a parent resource collection in the school library.

Family Support

1. Organize parenting education courses through the PTA which offer child care, car pools or other transportation assistance, and a sliding fee or scholarship fund for low-income parents.

2. Organize parents' support and children's support groups on the school's premises, training school counselors to run several time-limited groups per year. See Chapter Four for more information about several programs.

3. Encourage parents to organize their own single parent group at school through which parents can create their own support network, receive practical single-parenting advice and share child care duties.

4. Start a peer counseling program through which grandparents and high school students can "adopt" a younger student and show interest and concern, or provide such a school program through community organizations such as Big Sisters and Big Brothers.

5. Train all school personnel to respond with a nonjudgmental, caring attitude to parents and children in a family crisis, remembering how hard it may be for family members to communicate with the school during such periods.

School-Based Child Care

1. Survey parents about their child care program preferences. Some parents may be willing to pay for organized recreational activities while others may prefer a more comprehensive program after school that includes tutoring assistance and in-door activities as well. Still other parents may require an early morning breakfast program in addition to an after-school program.

2. Offer child care on a sliding scale or scholarship fund basis so that parents who cannot afford private care do not have to leave their children alone at home. If school resources and parent contributions are insufficient to fund a school program, then work with community agencies to offer a community-based program on school premises.

3. Provide "latchkey survival training" as part of the elementary school curriculum. All children, regardless of their child care status, can benefit from learning how to answer the telephone when alone at home, how to get help during an emergency, how to work safely in the kitchen, and how to play or study creatively alone.

Classroom Activities

1. Provide an open, warm atmosphere that respects non-traditional families. This can be fostered in several ways:

- Teach a special unit on different types of families.
- Make material (books, filmstrips, etc.) available about families, avoiding texts of family stereotypes.
- Encourage students to talk about their families, while being sensitive to students who do not want classmates to know about their family status.
- Bring general discussions about one-parent families into the classroom.

2. Help single parents get involved in their child's education.

- Set long deadlines for homework so that parents can plan to be available to assist, if necessary.
- Send home a weekly or monthly homework schedule so that parents and children can better plan their homework time.
- Inform both custodial and non-custodial parents about the child's progress and about special school events.
- Do not overload a parent with school obligations, but encourage the parent to stay in touch with the school and be involved as time permits.
- Help parents become better tutors by offering them structured home-learning activities to do with their children.
- Schedule school events when working parents can attend.
- Provide child care during parent/teacher conferences.

3. Be consistent with the students, but flexible at times when a child is clearly pressured by family problems. Set limits in order to prevent manipulative behavior from students, but be sensitive to a child's family situation.

BIBLIOGRAPHY

Adams, Paul L.; Milner, Judith R.; and Schrepf, Nancy A. *Fatherless Children*. New York: John Wiley & Sons, 1984.

Amato, Paul R. "Family Processes in One-Parent, Stepparent, and Intact Families: The Child's Point of View." *Journal of Marriage and the Family*, May, 1987, pp. 327–337.

Amato, Paul R., and Partridge, Sonia. "Widows and Divorcées With Dependent Children: Material, Personal, Family and Social Well-Being." *Family Relations*, July, 1987, pp. 316–320.

Appel, Karen W. "America's Changing Families: A Guide for Educators." *Fastback 219*. Phi Delta Kappa Educational Foundation, 1985.

Arendell, Teresa Jane. "Lives of Quiet Desperation: Divorced Women With Children." Unpublished Ph.D. dissertation, Graduate Division, University of California, Berkeley, 1984.

Beckwith, Helen K.; Miller, Susan; Morris, Tina; and Sage, Karyl. *Schools and the Changing Family: How the Schools Can Better Meet the Needs of Children From the Varying Family Structures That Exist Today*. Oneonta, New York: 1986.

Beller, Andrea H., and Chung, Seung Sin. "The Impact of Child Support Payments on the Educational Attainment of Children." Prepared for presentation at the Population Association of America Annual Meeting, New Orleans, April 21, 1988.

Beller, Andrea H., and Grahm, John W. "Child Support Awards: Differentials and Trends by Race and Marital Status." *Demography*, May, 1986, pp. 231–244.

Benedek, Richard S., and Benedek, Elissa P. "Children of Divorce: Can We Meet Their Needs?" *Journal of Social Issues,* 1979, pp. 155–169.

Bilge, Barbara, and Kaufman, Gladis. "Children of Divorce and One-Parent Families: Cross-cultural Perspectives." *Family Relations,* January, 1983, pp. 59–71.

Blechman, Elaine A. "Are Children with One Parent at Psychological Risk? A Methodological Review." *Journal of Marriage and the Family,* February, 1982, pp. 179–195.

Britton, Gwyneth; Lumpkin, Margaret; and Britton, Esther. "The Battle to Imprint Citizens for the 21st Century." *The Reading Teacher,* April, 1984, pp. 724–733.

Brooks, Andrea. "Divorced Parents and School Notices." *The New York Times,* March 7, 1984, C1, p. 14.

Brooks, Andrea. "Divorced Parents and the Neglected Child." *The New York Times,* July 28, 1986, B5, p. 7.

Brown, Frank B. "A Study of the School Needs of Children from One-Parent Families." *Phi Delta Kappan,* April, 1980, pp. 537–540.

Burns, Christine W., and Brassard, Marla R. "A Look at the Single Parent Family: Implications for the School Psychologist." *Psychology in the Schools,* October, 1982, pp. 487–494.

Calabrese, Raymond L.; Miller, John W.; and Dooley, Buddy. "The Identification of Alienated Parents and Children: Implications for School Psychologists." *Psychology in the Schools,* April, 1987, pp. 145–150.

Chase, Richard A., et al. "Single Parent Families: A Needs Assessment Survey of Single Parents, Ramsey County, Minnesota." St. Paul: Amhearst H. Wilder Foundation, December, 1985.

Chase-Lansdale, Lindsay, and Hetherington, E. Mavis. "The Impact of Divorce on Life-span Development: Short and Longterm Effects." To appear in D. L. Featherman and R. M. Lerner (eds.), *Life-span Development and Behavior.*

Clay, Phyllis L. "School Policy in Observing Rights of Noncustody Parents." *The Education Digest,* January, 1981, pp. 21–22.

Clay, Phyllis L. "Single Parents and the Public Schools: How Does the Partnership Work?" Results of a National Survey by the National Committee for Citizens in Education, 1981.

Committee for Economic Development. Research and Policy Committee. *Children in Need: Investment Strategies for the Educationally Disadvantaged.* New York: Committee for Economic Development, 1987.

Conroy, Mary. "After-School Programs for Kids." *Better Homes and Gardens,* August 1988.

Conway, Grace, and Mechler, Geraldine. "A Study of How Basal Readers Reflect Family Living Styles." Unpublished M.A. thesis, Kean College of New Jersey, April, 1983.

Dawson, Terry. "Safety Pals Available to California's Schools." *Thrust,* May/June, 1987, pp. 42–43.

Delaney, Elaine; Richards, Jane E.; and Strathe, Marlene I. "A Study of the Single-Parent Child in the Catholic School." *Momentum,* December, 1984, pp. 41–43.

Devall, Esther; Soneman, Zolinda; and Brody, Gene. "The Impact of Divorce and Maternal Employment on Pre-adolescent Children." *Family Relations,* January, 1986, pp. 153–159.

Diamond, Susan Arnsberg. *Helping Children of Divorce: A Handbook for Parents and Teachers.* New York: Schocken Books, 1985.

Drake, Ellen A. "Children of Separation and Divorce: A Review of School Programs and Implications for the Psychologist." *School Psychology Review,* 1981, pp. 54–61.

Drake, Ellen A. "Helping Children Cope With Divorce: The Role of the School." *Children of Separation and Divorce: Management and Treatment.* Edited by Irving R. Stuart and Lawrence Edwin Abt. New York: Van Nostrand Reinhold Co., 1981.

Ellwood, David T. *Poor Support: Poverty in the American Family.* New York: Basic Books, Inc., 1988.

Elmore, L. Joanne. "The Teacher and the Child of Divorce." Paper presented at the Annual Families Alive Conference, September, 1986.

Epstein, Joyce L. "Single Parents and the Schools: The Effect of Marital Status on Parent and Teacher Evaluations." Baltimore: Johns Hopkins University Center for the Study of Social Organization of Schools, March, 1984.

Epstein, Joyce L. "Toward a Theory of Family—School Connections: Teacher Practices and Parent Involvement." *Social Intervention: Potential and Constraints.* Edited by Klaus Hurrelmann, Franz-Xaver Kaufmann, and Friedrich Losel. Berlin: Walter de Gruyter, 1987.

Epstein, Joyce L. "What Principals Should Know About Parent Involvement." *Principal,* January, 1986.

Fiske, Edward B. "New York's Chancellor Seeks To Broaden Teachers' Roles." *The New York Times,* August 22, 1988, A1.

Fuller, Mary Lou. "Teachers' Perceptions of Children from Intact and Single-Parent Families." *The School Counselor,* May, 1986, pp. 365–373.

Fuller, Mary Lou. "Teachers' Perceptions of Parents from Intact and Single-Parent Families." *Educational Horizons,* Spring, 1984, pp. 94–95.

Furstenburg, Frank F., Jr. and Nord, Christine Winquist. "Parenting Apart: Patterns of Childbearing After Marital Disruption." *Journal of Marriage and the Family,* November, 1985, pp. 893–904.

Furstenburg, Frank F., Jr.; Nord, Christine Winquist; Peterson, James L.; and Zill, Nicholas. "The Life Course of Children of Divorce: Marital Disruption and Parental Contact." *American Sociological Review,* October, 1983, pp. 656–668.

Garfinkel, Irwin, and McLanahan, Sarah S. *Single Mothers and Their Children: A New American Dilemma.* Washington, DC: The Urban Institute Press, 1986.

Gladow, Nancy Wells, and Ray, Margaret P. "The Impact of Informal Support Systems on the Well Being of Single Parents." *Family Relations,* January, 1986, pp. 113–123.

Goldstein, Alan. "Establishing a Group Counseling Program for Elementary School Children Who Have Experienced Parental Divorce." Unpublished Ed.D. practicum, Nova University, 1985.

Green, Barbara J. "Helping Single-Parent Families." *Elementary School Guidance & Counseling.* February, 1981, pp. 249–261.

Greenleaf, Barbara Kaye, with Schaffer, Lewis A. *Help: A Handbook for Working Mothers.* New York: Thomas Y. Crowell, 1978.

Guidubaldi, John; Cleminshaw, Helen K.; Perry, Joseph D.; Nastasi, Bonnie K.; and Lightel, Jeanine. "The Role of Selected Family Environment Factors in Children's Post-Divorce Adjustment." *Family Relations,* January, 1986, pp. 141–151.

Gwynn, Carol A., and Brantley, Helen T. "Effects of a Divorce Group Intervention for Elementary School Children." *Psychology in the Schools,* April, 1987, pp. 161–164.

Hammond, Janice M. "Children of Divorce: A Study of Self-Concept, Academic Achievement and Attitudes." *The Elementary School Journal,* November, 1979, pp. 55–62.

Hanson, Shirley M. H. "Healthy Single Parent Families." *Family Relations,* January, 1986, pp. 125–132.

Hare, Jan, et al. "The Child in Grief: Implications for Teaching." Paper presented at the Annual Meeting of the National Council on Family Relations, San Francisco, October, 1984.

Harris, Louis, and Associates. *The American Teacher 1987: Strengthening Links Between Home and School.* Survey conducted for Metropolitan Life Insurance Company. New York: Louis Harris and Associates, 1987.

"Help for Single Parents: Agencies and Organizations." *Family Relations,* January, 1986, pp. 213–214.

Henderson, Anne T.; et al. *Beyond the Bake Sale: An Educator's Guide to Working with Parents.* Washington, DC: Catholic University of America, 1986.

Hetherington, E. Mavis. "Coping With Family Transitions: Winners, Losers, and Survivors." *Child Development,* in press.

Hetherington, E. Mavis; Camara, Kathleen A.; and Featherman, David L. "Achievement and Intellectual Functioning of Children in One-Parent Households." *Achievement and Achievement Motives.* San Francisco: W. H. Freeman, 1983.

Hetherington, E. Mavis; Hagan, Margaret Stanley; and Anderson, Edward R. "Marital Transitions: A Child's Perspective." American Psychological Institute, in press.

Hess, Robert D., and Camara, Kathleen A. ."Post-Divorce Family Relationships as Mediating Factors in the Consequences of Divorce for Children." *Journal of Social Issues,* 1979, pp. 79–96.

Hughs, Robert, Jr. and Scherer, Jane A. (Coordinators). "Parenting on Your Own." A series of thirteen guides prepared for the University of Illinois at Urbana-Champaign, College of Agriculture, Cooperative Extension Service, Circulars 1245–1258, 1986.

Ihinger-Tallman, Marilyn. "Member Adjustment in Single-Parent Families: Family Building." *Family Relations,* January, 1986, pp. 215–221.

Isaacs, Marla Beth; Leon, George H.; and Donohue, Ann Marie. "Who Are the 'Normal' Children of Divorce? On the Need to Specify A Population." *Journal of Divorce,* Summer, 1987, pp. 107–119.

Isaacs, Marla Beth, and Leon, George H. "Social Networks, Divorce, and Adjustment: A Tale of Three Generations." *Journal of Divorce,* Summer, 1986, pp. 1–16.

Kealey, Robert J. "The Image of the Family in Second Grade Readers." *Momentum,* October, 1980, pp. 16–19.

Kelly, Joan B. "Myths and Realities for Children of Divorce." *Educational Horizons,* Fall, 1980, pp. 34–39.

Keniston, Kenneth, and The Carnegie Council on Children. *All Our Children: The American Family Under Pressure.* New York: Harcourt Brace Jovanovich, 1977.

Kennedy, Mary M.; Jung, Richard K.; and Orland, Martin E. "Poverty, Achievement and the Distribution of Compensatory Education Services." An Interim Report from the National Assessment of Chapter 1, Office of Educational Research and Improvement, U.S. Department of Education, January, 1986.

Knight, Bryan M. *Enjoying Single Parenthood.* Toronto: Van Nostrand Reinhold Ltd., 1980.

Krein, Sheila Fitzgerald. "Growing Up in a Single Parent Family: The Effect on Education and Earnings of Young Men." *Family Relations,* January, 1986, pp. 161–168.

Krein, Sheila Fitzgerald, and Beller, Andrea H. "Educational Attainment of Children From Single Parent Families: Differences by Exposure, Gender, and Race." *Demography,* May, 1988, pp. 221–234.

Krementz, Jill. *How It Feels When a Parent Dies.* New York: Alfred A. Knopf, Inc., 1981.

Krementz, Jill. *How it Feels When Parents Divorce.* New York: Alfred A. Knopf, Inc., 1981.

Levitin, Teresa E. "Children of Divorce: An Introduction." *Journal of Social Issues,* 1979, pp. 1–25.

Lightfoot, Sara Lawrence. *The Good High School: Portraits of Character and Culture.* New York: Basic Books, Inc., 1983.

Linney, Jean Ann, and Vemberg, Eric. "Changing Patterns of Parental Employment and the Family-School Relationship." *Children of Working Parents: Experience and Outcomes.* Washington, DC: National Academy Press, 1983.

McGann, John, and Strauss, Jane. "Building a Network for Children of Divorce." Paper presented at the National Association of Social Workers, New Orleans, January-February, 1985.

McLanahan, Sara S. "Family Structure and Dependency: Early Transitions to Female Family Headship." Institute for Research on Poverty Discussion, paper no. 807–86, March, 1986.

Milne, Ann M.; Myers, David E.; Rosenthal, Alvin S.; and Ginsburg, Alan. "Single Parents, Working Mothers, and the Educational Achievement of School Children." *Sociology of Education,* July, 1986, pp. 125–129.

Mincer, Jullian. "L.I. Counselor Helps Children Deal With Shock of Divorce." *The New York Times,* July 1, 1985.

"Montour: More than Education." Unpublished report prepared by the Montour School District, McKees Rocks, PA, 1986.

Moore, Kristin, A.; Peterson, James L.; and Zill, Nicholas. "Family Types: Children Living with Fathers, with Divorced or Separated Mothers, or With a Mother Who Was Unmarried at Their Birth." Paper prepared under Grant HD-19380, Demographic and Behavioral Sciences Branch, NICHD, Revised June, 1987.

Moore, Nancy E., and Sumner, Margaret G. "Support Group for Children of Divorce: A Family Life Enrichment Group Model." Paper presented at the Annual Meeting of the National Association of Social Workers, New Orleans, January–February, 1985.

Nelson, Geoffrey. "Coping with the Loss of a Father: Family Reaction to Death or Divorce." *Journal of Family Issues*, March, 1982, pp. 41–60.

Newberger, Carolyn Moore; Melnicoe, Lora H.; and Newberger, Eli H. "The American Family in Crisis: Implications for Children." *Current Problems in Pediatrics*, 1986, pp. 673–721.

Norton, Arthur J., and Glick, Paul C. "One Parent Families: A Social and Economic Profile." *Family Relations*, January, 1986, pp. 9–17.

Ourth, John, and Zakariya, Sally Banks. "The School and the Single Parent Student: What Schools Can Do to Help." *Principal*, September, 1982, pp. 24–38.

Pedro-Carroll, JoAnne, and Cowen, Emory L. "The Children of Divorce Intervention Program: An Investigation of the Efficacy of a School-Based Prevention Program," *Journal of Consulting and Clinical Psychology*, 1985.

Pedro-Carroll, JoAnne; Cowen, Emory L.; Hightower, A. Dirk; and Guare, John C. "Preventative Intervention with Latency-Aged Children of Divorce: A Replication Study." *American Journal of Community Psychology*, 1986.

Pedro-Carroll, JoAnne, and Alpert-Gillis, Linda. "A Conceptual Model of Preventive Interventions for Children of Divorce." Paper presented at the 96th Annual Convention of the American Psychological Association, Atlanta, Georgia, 1988.

Pedro-Carroll, JoAnne. *The Children of Divorce Intervention Program Procedures Manual.* Rochester: University of Rochester, 1987.

Peterson, James L. "The Effects of Marital Disruption on Children." Statement prepared for the hearings of the House Select Committee on Children, Youth, and Families on "Divorce: The Impact on Children and Families." Washington, DC, July, 1986.

Peterson, James L. "A National Longitudinal Study of Marital Disruption." Prepared for Child Trends, Inc., March, 1984.

Peterson, James L., and Zill, Nicholas. "Marital Disruption, Parent-Child Relationships, and Behavior Problems in Children." *Journal of Marriage and the Family,* May 1986, pp. 295–307.

Phelps, Randy E., and Huntley, Debra K. "Social Networks and Child Adjustment in Single-Parent Families." Paper presented at the Annual Convention of the American Psychological Association, Los Angeles, August, 1985.

Press-Dawson, Andee. "Unlocking the Latchkey Problem." *Thrust,* May/June, 1987, pp. 40–41.

Prinz, Ronald J., et al. "Children of Separating Parents: They Are Not All Alike." Paper presented at the Annual Convention of the American Psychological Association, Anaheim, August, 1983.

Randall, Kay L. "The Single-Parent Child in the Classroom." Annotated Bibliography, June, 1981.

Rich, Dorothy. "Megaskills: How Families Can Help Children Learn in School and Beyond." Home and School Institute, Special Projects Office, 1988.

Robinson, Bryan E.; Rowland, Bobbie H.; and Coleman, Mick. "Taking Action for Latchkey Children and Their Families." *Family Relations,* October, 1986, pp. 473–478.

Robinson, Bryan E.; Rowland, Bobbie H.; and Coleman, Mick. *Latchkey Kids: Unlocking Doors for Children and Their Families.* Toronto: Lexington Books, 1986.

Rodgers, Harrell R., Jr. *Poor Women, Poor Families: The Economic Plight of America's Female-Headed Households.* Armonk, NY: M. E. Sharpe, Inc., 1986.

Rodman, Hyman, and Cole, Cynthia. "Latchkey Children: A Review of Policy and Resources." *Family Relations,* January, 1987, pp. 101–105.

Sanik, Margaret Mietus, and Maudlin, Teresa. "Single Versus Two-Parent Families: A Comparison of Mothers' Time." *Family Relations,* January, 1986, pp. 53–56.

Santrock, John W., and Tracy, Russel L. "Effects of Children's Family Structure Status on the Development of Stereotypes by Teachers." *Journal of Educational Psychology,* 1978, pp. 754–757.

Schlesinger, Benjamin. "Single Parent Families: A Bookshelf: 1978–1985." *Family Relations,* January, 1986, pp. 199–204.

Schlesinger, Benjamin. *The One-Parent Family in the 1980's: Perspectives and Annotated Bibliography, 1978–1984.* Toronto: University of Toronto Press, 1985.

"Schools, Single Parents and Their Children." Compilation of Policy Suggestions prepared by Parents Without Partners, Inc., Silver Spring, MD.

Schorr, Lisbeth, B., with Schorr, Daniel. *Within Our Reach: Breaking the Cycle of Disadvantage.* New York: Anchor Press, 1988.

Sherman, Beth. "Helping the Children of Divorce." *The New York Times,* April 14, 1985, B20.

Single Parents and Their Families: A Guide to Involving School And Community. Guide prepared by the National PTA, Boys Town, and the National Association of Elementary School Principals, 1983.

Stedman, James B. "The Educational Attainment of Select Groups of 'At Risk' Children and Youth." *Congressional Research Service,* Report No. 87-920, Library of Congress, April 1, 1987.

Stedman, James B.; Salganik, Laura Hersh; and Celebuski, Carin A. "Dropping Out: The Educational Vulnerability of At-Risk Youth."

CRS Report for Congress. Congressional Research Service, Library of Congress, May 24, 1988.

Stolberg, Arnold L.; Zacharias, Michael A.; and Camplair, Christopher W. *Children's Support Group: Kids Book.* Manual prepared for the Divorce Adjustment Project, Department of Psychology, Virginia Commonwealth University, 1988.

Sumrak, Sherry M. *An Annotated Bibliography of the Literature Dealing with the Effect of Divorce on School Age Children and How Schools Can Meet Their Needs.* April, 1984.

Touliatos, John, and Lindholm, Byron W. "Teachers' Perceptions of Behavior Problems in Children from Intact, Single-Parent, and Stepparent Families." *Psychology in the Schools,* 1980, pp. 264–269.

True, Judy, and Googins, Duane. "Extended Learning Opportunities for the Single Parent Family." Paper presented at the National Reading and Language Arts Educator's Conference, Kansas, September, 1984.

U.S. Department of Commerce, Bureau of the Census. "Fertility of American Women: June 1987." *Current Population Reports,* Series P-20, No. 427.

U.S. Department of Commerce, Bureau of the Census. "Household and Family Characteristics: March 1987." *Current Population Reports,* Series P-20, No. 424.

U.S. Department of Commerce, Bureau of the Census. "Marital Status and Living Arrangements: March 1987." *Current Population Reports,* Series P-20, No. 423.

U.S. Department of Commerce, Bureau of the Census. "Money, Income and Poverty Status of Families and Persons in the United States: 1986." *Current Population Reports,* Series P-60, No. 157.

U.S. Department of Commerce, Bureau of the Census. "School Enrollment—Social and Economic Characteristics of Students: October 1985 and 1984." *Current Population Reports,* Series P-20, No. 426.

U.S. Department of Commerce, Bureau of the Census. "Who's Minding the Kids? Child Care Arrangements: Winter 1984–85." *Current Population Reports,* Series P-70, No. 9.

U.S. Department of Labor. *Child Care: A Workforce Issue.* Report of the Secretary's Task Force, April, 1988.

Walker, Alexis, J.; Martin, Sally S.; Kees, Martin; and Thompson, Linda. "Feminist Programs for Families." *Family Relations,* January, 1988, pp. 17–22.

Wallerstein, Judith S., and Kelly, Joan Berlin. *Surviving the Breakup: How Children and Parents Cope with Divorce.* New York: Basic Books, Inc., 1980.

Weiss, Robert S. *Going It Alone: The Family Life and Social Situation of the Single Parent.* New York: Basic Books, Inc., 1979.

Weitzman, Lenore J. *The Divorce Revolution: The Unexpected Social and Economic Consequences for Women and Children in America.* New York: The Free Press, 1985.

Wilken, Ronald L. *Missouri Public Schools and the Single-Parent Family.* Ann Arbor, MI: University Microfilms International, 1987.

Wilkinson, Gary S., and Blek, Robert. "Children's Divorce Groups." *Elementary School Guidance and Counseling,* February, 1977, pp. 205–213.

Worell, Judith. "Single Mothers: Issues of Stigma." Paper presented at the Annual Convention of the American Psychological Association, Washington, DC, August, 1986.

Zill, Nicholas, and Rogers, Carolyn C. "Recent Trends in the Well Being of Children in the United States and Their Implications for Public Policy." In: Andrew Cherlin (editor), *Family Change and Public Policy.* Washington, DC: The Urban Institute Press, 1988.

INDEX